You're NOT Lifting Your Head

By

Charlie King

UnCommon golf™

You're NOT Lifting Your Head
By Charlie King
©2000 by Charlie King

Published by UnCommon Golf
P.O. Box 181124
Casselberry FL 32718-1124

Editing by A+ WRITING
Cover design by INFINITE IDEAS & DESIGNS
Illustrations by Bob Dellinger

Printed in the United States of America

ISBN: 0-9674101-0-3
Library of Congress Number Pending
Price: $15.00

Cataloging-in-Publication Data

King, Charles, 1964-
You're NOT Lifting Your Head/by Charlie King
    p.cm.
ISBN: 0-9674010-0-3
    1. Golf. 2. Golf techniques. 3. Golfers, American.   I. Title
                                                                CIP

Here's What People are Saying About . . .
You're NOT Lifting Your Head

"As an instructor and coach for 50 years, I can tell you that there is no better book than *You're NOT Lifting Your Head*, and there's no better authority and teacher than Charlie King. Golfers should have been told this years ago."

Coach Conrad Rehling, *Golf Magazine* Top 100 Teacher
Golf coach for Jerry Pate, Bob Murphy, and Steve Lowery

"Charlie [teaches] these concepts every day at the Golf Academy of the South, and they work. He is an extremely dedicated teacher. I went from a 15-handicap to a 3-handicap. You're cheating yourself if you don't read this book."

Mike Sullivan, PGA Apprentice
Golf Academy of the South graduate

"This book is for the frustrated masses who want to learn this game. I've taken 15 shots off my game with Charlie's help."

Nancy Harvey, Golf Academy of the South Graduate

"My first semester as a TGAS student I shot a 127 in a tournament. By the time I left 16 months later I had shot a 78 in a tournament and a 75 in a casual round. I have since passed the PGA playing ability test by shooting a 76 and a 77 in back-to-back rounds. Charlie gave me a firm understanding of the fundamentals of golf and he was my coach. Not only did my game get better, but I am now transferring these correct concepts to my students."

Chuck Goller, PGA Apprentice
Golf Academy of the South graduate

"I've worked alongside Charlie for eight years, and he absolutely wants you to get better so you can enjoy golf more. I have personally witnessed the multitude of golfers that have improved because of his understandable instruction. He has written a book that is easy to understand, and if you follow what it says, your improvement is guaranteed!"

Brad Turner, PGA Professional
Campus Director, The Golf Academy of the South

"With Charlie's help, I was able to qualify for the 1999 U.S. Amateur at Pebble Beach. This was a big thrill, and I was able to post a 71 in tough conditions at Pebble Beach the second day, which was the low score of the day. What Charlie teaches works."

Nik Desai, Golf Academy of the South graduate

Contents

Illustrations

vi

About the Author

CHARLIE KING GREW UP IN THE EAST TENNESSEE TOWN of Decatur. He was bitten by the golf bug while a student at Tennessee Technological University. After graduating with a

B.S. in Marketing in 1987, he pursued his dream of being a player in Orlando, Florida. He searched for a teacher who would help him reach his full potential, but was unsuccessful the first few years. Charlie quickly learned his passion was not limited to playing, but that he found a similar enjoyment in teaching others to maximize their potential. His difficulty in finding a teacher for his own game during this period inspired him to write an understandable book that would enable other golfers to avoid these same pitfalls and identify a competent professional.

Charlie began his career in 1988 as an assistant professional and then as a teaching professional at Swing's the Thing Golf Schools at Orange Lake Country Club. Since 1992, he has taught at The Golf Academy of the South. He takes great pride in helping the current students and graduates achieve their own dreams in the golf industry. He has served as the Education

Chairman for the East Central Chapter of the PGA since 1995 and was the recipient of the North Florida Horton Smith Award from his chapter and section of the PGA for his contributions to education.

This book marks the beginning of Charlie's efforts to see fundamental change in the way golfers approach learning golf. He believes that more people could enjoy this game of all games more fully if they only knew how. In establishing his company, UnCommon Golf, he is taking his passion for seeing improvement in his students' games to a higher level with the book, an Internet site and a newsletter.

He lives in Orlando, Florida, with his wife, Julie, and daughter, Kathryn.

Acknowledgments

THERE IS A LOT THAT GOES INTO THE PRODUCTION of a book—more than I had imagined. I extend my thanks to those who have directly influenced this book.

To my wife Julie for her love and support throughout the writing process, and my daughter, Kathryn, for the inspiration.

To my mom and dad for the values and work ethic they instilled in me.

To my teaching mentors. Harry Obitz for showing me clubface positions at the top and challenging me as a young teacher. Craig Shankland for caring about whether I got better or not and for showing me the effect of energy and enthusiasm on your students. Coach Conrad Rehling for crystallizing teaching in progression, skill testing, short game, and "coaching" golfers. Dick Farley for teaching me about swing plane, and for those long drives between golf schools listening to Harry Bradshaw and Homer Kelley. Rick McCord for giving me an opportunity to learn to teach. Mike Bender for his ideas on drills and training aids, as well as working with me to refine my golf swing.

To my great friend Scottie Griffin for his untiring efforts in proofreading, editing and rewriting of the manuscript of this book.

To my friend and colleague at TGAS, Brad Turner, for the many talks over the years that have influenced my thoughts on playing, teaching and the short game.

To Rae Taylor for her tremendous help in editing and proofreading.

To the many people who have proofread the text and made contributions to the final product. There are too many to mention by name, but I know who you are.

To the people at INFINITE IDEAS & DESIGNS for the superior cover design and the many helpful hints on self-publishing a book.

To Drollene P. Brown of A+ WRITING for copy-editing and typesetting the book and for her professionalism throughout the process.

To Bob Dellinger for a fantastic job on the illustrations.

To Mike Sullivan and Derek Dirnberger for serving as models for the illustrations.

Introduction

How MANY OF YOU WANT TO GET BETTER? Okay, you can put your hands down. I know the answer. All of us want to get better. And as well as getting better, we would like to have a clue as to why we hit bad shots. In this book, you will be along for the ride as J.B. Hawkins tries to figure out how to get better and where his bad shots come from.

Wouldn't it be great to stop topping the ball, hitting behind the ball, and slicing it? These very problems have driven golfers to desperate measures for years. My questions to you are: Why are these problems so common? And how come, no matter how hard you try, they keep coming back? The answer is **misconceptions**. A misconception is something that we picture and believe, even though it is incorrect. By practicing with a misconception, we develop bad habits that lead to poor results. My job as a teacher is to fill your mind with correct concepts and ideas; only when this happens will you have a chance to reach your potential as a golfer.

Nothing hurts me more as a teacher than to watch people struggle in their golf games because of bad information and, consequently, bad habits. I know this feeling firsthand, because I learned golf the "wrong" way myself. Some friends took me to play for the first time when I was 19 years old. I considered it a victory that day just to make contact with the ball. These same friends gave me "tips" on how to play better, and I was able to "master" a slice for the next two years. I read golf magazines and books and watched videos; by my third year, I was thoroughly confused. I had a friend who then showed me how to hook the ball, and I played with a chronic hook for the next few years.

Despite these frustrations, I had the golf bug to the point that I decided to see just how good I could become as a golfer. I sought out a teacher and had a bad experience similar to the one J.B. Hawkins has with Jack Pierce in this book. I came to Florida for a career in the golf business and to find someone to help me reach my potential as a player. Instead of the method instruction that I had received in my first lesson experience, I got lessons with no cohesiveness at all. I struggled with my game and considered quitting several times. Finally, however, I ran into a series of fantastic teachers who helped me in the development of my game: Harry Obitz, Craig Shankland, Conrad Rehling, Brad Turner and Mike Bender. There were others who influenced my thinking about teaching and the methods I employ: Dave Rhone, Jay Bowden, Chuck Cook, Jerry Tucker, Dick Farley, Rick McCord and Carl Rabito.

The things I learned as a player and new teacher have led to what I know and believe as an experienced teacher today. I am convinced that if you are serious about the game of golf, you should find a qualified golf instructor as soon as you can, because this instructor will cut your learning time down and make sure you have habits that lead to enjoyable golf.

Something that you will learn from this book is the importance of concepts. I have been amazed as a teacher at the number of misconceptions floating around golf as though they were the fundamentals. "You lifted your head," as the title of the book implies, is my least favorite. In my 11 years as a teacher, I have never seen anybody do it! Harry Wilkinson hits on this point in detail in this book. Keep your mind open to the correct concept that he teaches. The misconception that one should "Take the club straight through to the target," coupled with players' having poor grips, has led to an epidemic of slicing. We could rid the game of slicing if enthusiasts knew they must go to a qualified instructor. I challenge you to get rid of your slice this year!

I am absolutely committed to changing the fact that the majority of golfers are handicapped by these misconceptions. Every golfer deserves to get the right ideas and then see how good he or she can become. It's such a shame to watch golfers struggle because they have never been taught fundamentally sound concepts.

This book marks the beginning of my efforts—with the formation of UNCOMMON GOLF—to bring fundamental change to the way golf is taught and learned. Over the coming years, we are going to provide understandable books, affordable programs and, eventually, certified instructors near you with a staff that provides you with the correct concepts, proper feedback and coaching that you desire and need.

In this book, I have taken the "novel approach," which has been successful in communicating ideas in other arenas, such as personal finance (*The Wealthy Barber* and *The Richest Man In Babylon*), management (*The One Minute Manager*), and sales (*The Greatest Salesman in the World*). Through the situations and characters in this book, I hope you see a little bit of yourself and the solution to your golf problems.

By the end of this book you should:

>Understand the main reason for your mis-hits.

>Understand why you slice (or hook).

>Know that finding a qualified golf instructor, who will put you on a program, is the answer.

>Know what a qualified golf instructor is so you can find one and start getting better now!

1

The Last Straw

"I HATE THIS GAME," J.B. Hawkins shouted as his ball dribbled slowly and pitifully off the front of the tee. He kicked at his tee and swung his golf club at the air in disgust. Actually he loved the game. He just couldn't play it very well.

A light breeze ruffled the vibrant autumn leaves on the stately live oaks lining the fairways of South Knoxville's Ironwood Country Club. A freshly-loosened cluster of leaves fluttered down among the Southern pines before descending to the green velvet grass below. The cool, crisp fall morning was perfect for an early round, but J.B. didn't seem to notice. He was wrapped up in how bad his game was.

J.B. was not at one with nature right now. All he could feel was that pain again. It wasn't the same kind of pain he felt when his back became tight or his shoulder throbbed. This pain was deeper and more all encompassing. It flared up only on Saturdays during the golf season. And although J.B. had no real medical training, he easily diagnosed his ailment. It was his golf game.

"Keep your head down, J.B.," his best friend and golf partner, Brian Ahrens, admonished for possibly the thousandth time this year. It had been the same old litany between the two since Brian first took him out to play in college. J.B. figured this had to be golf's most common piece of advice.

"I *am* keeping my head down," J.B. shot back. "If there's *one* thing I do right, it's keep my eye on the ball." Even more irritated now, he sliced his next shot way off to the right.

Brian shook his head as they both watched the ball land in a clump of pine needles in the trees, 30 yards from the fairway. J.B.'s frustration was now reaching its boiling point, and they were only at the fifth hole.

Smiling, Brian needled, "You know, if you would just listen to me, you might keep it on the golf course." He stepped up for his tee shot, and the two men paused in their conversation as Brian took his shot. A lefty, Brian watched as his ball faded more to the left than he had intended, but it still ended up on top of some fluffy grass in the rough.

"See what I mean?" He winked and gave his friend a playful shot to the ribs. "It just takes talent, and if we don't speed things up here, we'll miss the kickoff."

The "kickoff" referred to the big football game between their alma mater, the Tennessee Volunteers, and one of the school's rivals, the Georgia Bulldogs. The match up wasn't quite as intense as with Alabama or Florida, but it was important nonetheless. Brian slid his club into his bag, and the two quickly walked to where their tee shots had landed.

J.B.'s agitation had reached a peak in today's round. The pair had always been competitive, and it drove him nuts to keep losing to his buddy on the golf course. He could hold his own against Brian in other sports, like bowling and racquetball. And in basketball, he could beat Brian hands down, but J.B. had always taken a backseat when it came to golf. It was more than the competitiveness, even though that was a part of it. Truth was, he wanted to play the game well so he could enjoy it, and it was driving him crazy that he wasn't better at it.

No matter what he did, his game had not improved significantly since his second year of playing. The worst part was that he was addicted to golf. It was such an individual challenge. It's not that he didn't try; he just couldn't seem to make a breakthrough. *Today*, he would think before a round, *I'm going to break 90.* Before he finished all 18 holes, however, he was usually ready to give away his clubs and quit the game. Today was no different from all the rest and, as usual, Brian was liberal with his advice and his taunting.

Brian was the one who had introduced J.B. to golf in their freshman year at the University of Tennessee. A couple of whiffs, a bunch of tops, and a batch of slices later, J.B. had completed his first round and was hooked. But it wasn't until his senior year that the golf bug bit him hard. Since that time, J.B. had collected every imaginable training aid and gadget he could find. His life revolved around golf on Saturdays, with his family playing second fiddle on that day.

One of the highlights of his month was when his issue of *Golf Magazine* arrived. He would pore over its pages, find a great tip, and immediately head to the range to give it a try. However, his enthusiasm was always short-lived. Between the magazine's helpful hints and the myriad methods outlined in the instructional books lining his shelves, he wasn't sure whether to swing flat like Ben Hogan or more upright like Jack Nicklaus. He didn't know whether to swing smooth like Freddie Couples or quicker like Nick Price. He certainly wouldn't take lessons. After all, he had been playing for a long time, and one's "self-taught" status was a badge of honor among golfers.

J.B. ventured into the woods on the right to see what nightmare lie awaited him, while Brian lined up for his next shot. The beauty of the day, the majesty of the trees, and the sound of the many birds singing went unnoticed by J.B. as he wallowed in frustration. In fact, J.B. hadn't noticed much of anything since the round started. He had his mind set on improving his game, but how? He had just read in a magazine about having a routine. He had a routine all right—the wrong one. All he did was make a swing, watch it slice (if he was lucky to get it airborne), and then slam his club into the ground when the ball took off with a mind of its own.

Golf had a way of bringing out the worst in him. In other areas of his life, he had control over his emotions. He didn't even swear, but some of the words that came to mind on a bad golf day . . . Time and again, he watched other golfers lose it over a bad shot. He had seen it all. Guys stomping their feet, ranting and raving, and throwing their clubs straighter and farther than they hit the ball. In his rational moments, he thought to himself *Boy, do they look like idiots!* Then, in the throes of gut-wrenching frustration, he, too, would helicopter a club and stomp off to pick it up.

With the sun moving to its mid-morning position, the dew had long since evaporated from the fairways and greens of Ironwood, as had J.B.'s hopes for a great round of golf. His game had gone south after recording a quadruple bogie nine on the now infamous par five fifth hole. Not that he found any other hole friendly to him, but the fifth hole had his number. It was a dogleg left with water on the right and out-of-bounds on the left. As hard as he tried, he invariably hit his tee shot down the middle for the first 50 or 60 yards of its flight, then watched it slice violently toward the water. He would go over to check for his ball in the pond that so often had seen his disgusted reflection. The rest of the fifth hole's story varied slightly with each round, but it usually included a thin iron shot, a chunked chip, and a three-putt.

Today as the round continued, he could not get the fifth hole out of his mind. He snapped out of his daze momentarily as he stepped up to the fifteenth hole. With four holes to go, he was determined to do better. Searching through his mental Rolodex of golf instruction articles and videos, he hoped to salvage something. *Finish strong, swing smooth, you can do it*, were the thoughts on which he settled.

He gave the tee shot extra mental effort. For a fleeting moment, a ray of hope ran through him. He took a little more time to set up for the shot. As the club went back, he just said to himself, *Stay slow*. The club almost made it to the top when the urge to hit the ball came upon him. The muscles in his arms and hands tensed up, so much so that the effort had to be visible to anyone around him. In what can only be described as a whirlwind of effort, J.B. lunged violently at the helpless Top Flite sitting on an orange wooden tee. Losing his balance in the follow through, J.B. watched his shot curve like a foul ball to right field and spin off into the deep of the trees, glancing off one of the great oaks about 180 yards from the tee and bouncing out of sight.

That was the last straw! He lost what little composure he had left and began his version of a tirade by ripping the UT hat from his head and hurling it to the ground. He then motioned to throw the driver into the woods, but somehow managed to stop himself. His disgust drove him to internally shout a string of foul language that would have made a sailor blush. The self-serving pep talk hadn't helped him a bit. Was it no talent? Was it the clubs? Or could you just call it a string of bad luck? *What was it?* Why couldn't he be more consistent? Why couldn't he hit it farther? Maybe if he could improve his swing . . . At this point, who cared? He just knew he needed help. Brian didn't say a word. He knew not to.

Instead of finishing strong, J.B. was 10 over par on the final four, with a big fat triple bogey on the last hole. His score of 105 was his highest of the year. When the round was finished, J.B. mumbled to Brian, "I'll see you inside," picked up his bag and started for his car.

As he made his way to the parking lot, he stared at the calm, clear lake to the left of the eighteenth hole. Visions of throwing his clubs, bag and all, into that big, over-sized lake where he had lost so many golf balls crossed his frazzled mind. So did dropping to his knees and weeping like a child. Composing himself somewhat, he turned around and trudged toward his SUV. *What's the use?* he thought. *Why do I put myself through all of this?* He slammed his clubs into the back of his Explorer instead of the water, then headed to the clubhouse to hand over money to Brian again. This was it, though. This time he was giving up golf for good!

* * *

Inside the clubhouse, J.B. joined Brian at a corner table and sat down. Brian had ordered their usual round and the waitress, Sally, had already brought it to the table—sweet tea for J.B. and a beer for Brian. Sally smiled at J.B., but this friendly gesture couldn't bring him back from his pit of despair.

"I stink," J.B. said with a moan as he grabbed a handful of pretzels from the bowl on the table and shoved them into his mouth. He took a big gulp of the tea to wash them down.

"Come on, you just had a bad day," Brian said, trying to console his old friend.

"A bad day? I'm *always* having a bad day. I just can't play worth crap, that's all." J.B. pounded the table with his fist and grabbed another handful of pretzels.

"Let it go. It's just a game. Besides," Brian joked good-naturedly, "with all the practice in the world, you couldn't beat *me*. I'm the man!" He smiled across the table.

"Verrry funny! That makes me feel a lot better." Pointing out the window to the lake, J.B. declared despondently, "I'm thinking about taking my useless clubs and throwing them into that lake out there."

"Well the way you're playing, you'd probably miss the water," Brian deadpanned.

J.B. shook his head slowly from side to side and pulled at the rim of his hat, barely moving his lips as he muttered, "Keep going, you're on a roll!"

"Besides," Brian continued, laughing, "there's no room at the bottom of that lake for your clubs, 'cause it's filled with your golf balls!"

"Brian, do me a favor. Could you take off your red cape and

put down your pitchfork for one minute and just listen to me."

Determined to cheer up his buddy, Brian wouldn't give up. "Hey, come on, it's just a game, for Pete's sake. It's not the end of the world. Now, if the Vols lose to Georgia today, then *that* will be the end of the world!"

"Brian, you don't understand. This round was the last straw. I'm going to find something to help my game or I'm gonna quit golf altogether. There are too many fun things to do on a Saturday besides this!" J.B. sat back in his chair, took a big swig of iced tea, and adjusted his "Big Orange" cap.

"What are you doing tomorrow?" Brian asked, suddenly stern-faced.

"The usual. Church with Rachel and the kids in the morning, but I don't have anything planned for later in the day after lunch."

"How about meeting me at the range around two o'clock?" Brian proposed.

"For what? For more of the same help I've gotten from you for the last ten years?"

"Hey, what can I say? You're a slow learner. But if I can play this game, so can you. There's something you're doing wrong. We just have to find out what it is. Maybe it's mental. Maybe you need to concentrate more on your fundamentals. You said yourself that you haven't been practicing."

That's what J.B. liked about his buddy. He was always willing to go the extra mile.

"I've got to do *something*," J.B. replied, with a desperation in his voice he had never allowed Brian to hear before. "I'll meet you there at two."

"All right! Now, let's go watch the game. Hey, don't throw your clubs in that lake . . . yet."

J.B. shook his head. When it came to the way he played golf, he wasn't sure there was any hope for his game.

2

The Driving Range

THE WEATHER COULD NOT HAVE BEEN MORE PERFECT for the mood in which J.B. found himself. Ominous black clouds, unusual for this time of year, had begun rolling in while he and his old pal were in the club house, and now they made it impossible for the autumn sun to peek through. Upon arriving home, J.B. felt a real chill in the air, but it barely cooled the anger which still, one full hour after the nightmare round had ended, coursed through his veins.

The falling leaves filled the gutters of his family's little brick cottage, edging the roof line in yellows and reds. As he walked toward it, he thought their home seemed to be bracing for the storm. *Well, the one good thing about weather like this*, he thought to himself, *is no yardwork today*. J.B.'s feeling about yardwork was very clear. He didn't like anything about it. In fact, it ranked right up there with paying taxes and dental surgery as his least favorite activities. When the grass was high enough to lose the dog, J.B. would reluctantly drag out the mower.

Despite his frustration and despair with his golf game, J.B. Hawkins knew he was a very lucky man, living his version of the American Dream. He had married his college sweetheart, Rachel, and she had since given birth to his pride and joy. Pride was his son, Nick, who—J.B. was sure—had a shot at professional baseball. And joy referred to his five-year-old daughter Margaret, who had inherited her mother's beauty and energy. The family had moved to the little brick house when Margaret was a few months old. Now they were already looking for a full-sized house to replace their compact model.

Rachel kept the house immaculately clean, and some of their biggest arguments came over J.B.'s being, in Rachel's words, a slob. When she found clothes on the floor and food stains on the carpet, she let him hear about it. His usual counter was to call her a neat freak, though he was actually glad she was that way. She couldn't really help it, having neatness instilled in her by her traditional Southern mom.

Each spring, Rachel planted a small garden with tomatoes, cucumbers, and a special lettuce she used to make J.B.'s favorite salad. Around his birthday the lettuce would be just right. Combined with bacon and a special dressing, the fresh vegetables were a treat.

Margaret and Nick shared a room in the little house, one of the reasons the family needed a bigger home. With Margaret in kindergarten and Nick in second grade, they were close to demanding their private space. Margaret's side of their room was decorated in various shades of pink to enhance the display of her large and ever growing Barbie collection. Next to their bunk beds, Nick's newfound love of baseball was conveyed with Atlanta Braves souvenirs and posters on the wall. Nick knew the entire team roster, along with batting averages and runs batted in. He idolized Chipper Jones, the Braves' third baseman, and had his poster prominently displayed on the back of the bedroom door. J.B. loved the fact that Nick was excited about baseball. The two of them spent cherished time watching the games together and playing catch outside. J.B. couldn't really explain it, but he believed there was something about the game of baseball that could bring a family together—especially a father and a son. He wanted to take Nick golfing, but he really didn't want Nick to see him at his emotional worst.

Rachel often said she wondered where the time had gone. They both had enjoyed Nick and Margaret's toddler years and felt melancholy when thinking of their babies growing up. With both parents believing in the importance of having a parent stay at home full time for the children, they had decided that Rachel would quit her job. She had been a nurse at Baptist Hospital and really enjoyed her work, but both of them believed that being home to raise the children was of the highest calling.

To round out the happy family picture, J.B. brought home an English Bulldog, which the children named Tiny. She was a short-legged, fawn colored, drooling mound of loyalty and love. With no tail to wag, she showed her happiness by wagging her whole body.

J.B. had grown up loving sports, and he did okay in school. He kicked his studies in gear in college and received a degree in civil engineering to follow in the footsteps of his father. Working for the Tennessee Valley Authority, the federally run electric company, enabled J.B. to more than adequately provide for his family.

He had chosen golf as a lifelong source of recreation and fun. There was only one problem: golf was starting to give him ulcers. He couldn't understand. He was a pretty good athlete and had some success in other sports. Golf looked easy when he watched it on TV. You just take the club back and swing through to the target. How hard could that be? It seemed very simple. But it had not been simple for him.

J.B. was far from a world traveler, but he had been to many cities and towns throughout the country, and he and Rachel agreed that Knoxville was where they belonged. Southern hospitality was more than just an idea here; it was a way of life. He loved the surrounding countryside, with its picturesque rolling hills and ridges. All this, together with a twenty-minute drive to the grandeur of the Smoky Mountains, made East Tennessee a beautiful place to live. This time of the year, when the leaves changed, he and his family would take a trip down the Blue Ridge Parkway to behold the kaleidoscope of brilliant autumn color.

The crisp cool air and changing colors also signaled the beginning of football season—around these parts known as the religion of Tennessee Volunteer football. Six or seven Saturdays each autumn, Neyland Stadium would swell to the size of the fifth largest city in Tennessee. The sound of legendary sportscaster John Ward announcing, "It's football time in Tennessee!" and the playing of "Rocky Top" signaled that this revered time of year had once again come to "Big Orange" country.

Today as the kickoff approached, J.B. thought about the closing of the golf season. After all, winter was coming and there weren't many weekends of golf left. Most golfers felt the same way about this time of year. It was like the fisherman looking to catch the "big one"! The opportunities for a great round were dwindling, as were the chances to salvage a positive experience to share with friends at dinner parties, casual get-togethers, or the annual Christmas party.

Throughout the game, J.B. stewed. He was always jealous of the guys who had enjoyed rounds where everything had gone their way. They would tell the story of that round, hole by hole, as if they just got off the golf course. J.B. would listen intently, but he always thought to himself, *Why can't I ever have one of those days?* He had some highlights here and there, but they were always overshadowed by a slew of bogies, doubles and—the low point of each round—handing a gloating Brian the money from another lost bet.

"Are you going to mope around all afternoon? You've had that sour look on your face for the entire game." Rachel, arms folded across her chest, stood in front of the window. A light drizzle outside was the only reminder of the earlier storm.

"I'm just playing so bad I can't stand it," J.B. said as he turned back to the post game wrap-up.

"Maybe you shouldn't even play golf if it's going to get you like this all the time," Rachel commented. "Tennessee won the game today, and you didn't so much as crack a smile. I've never seen you get this bad."

"I know. I've never felt this bad about my game," J.B. replied as he flipped the channel back to golf. Tiger Woods was hitting a drive. The announcer mentioned that his coach, Butch Harmon, had been working with Tiger on his distance control with his short irons.

"I was getting better in college, but I've just stayed the same for the last five or six years."

"Let me get this straight. Tiger Woods, who—I hear—is the best golfer right now, has a coach. However, J.B. Hawkins has his college buddy Brian Ahrens to ask for advice," Rachel said sarcastically.

"That's how most people learn to play." J.B.'s defense sounded weak even to his own ears.

"So when its time for Margaret to learn to play the piano, you're going to teach her?" Rachel inquired.

"Of course not. Don't be silly," J.B. scoffed.

"You know as much about playing the piano as Brian knows about playing golf," Rachel continued.

"Yeah, but that's different." J.B. knew he was losing ground.

"How's it different?" Rachel didn't relent.

"I don't know." J.B. gave in to Rachel's perfect logic. In fact, Rachel's logic was always like a splash of cold water to his face, and he had learned to appreciate it. He made one last stab at his long-held position. "I've been thinking about taking lessons, but what if I pay the money and the guy messes me up?"

"Messes you up?" Rachel asked incredulously. "You shot 105 today! What are your choices? To continue playing like this and taking tips from Brian?" Sarcasm dripped from her voice.

"Not to mention losing to him, which drives me nuts," J.B. admitted.

"We definitely need to do something about that," his wife said with a smile and a wink.

"I'm meeting Brian at the Golden Tee tomorrow after church," J.B. added.

"The blind leading the blind," Rachel scolded.

"Okay, okay!" He raised his arms in surrender. "I get the point. I'll think about it. The pro at the Golden Tee is supposed to be good. His name is Jack Pierce, I think."

* * *

The Golden Tee Driving Range was an old haunt for J.B. and Brian. Here it was that 15-handicapper Brian had shown J.B. his version of "the fundamentals" during their college years.

"Keep your head down."

"You lifted up on that one."

"Keep your left arm straight."

"Take it low and slow."

"Slow down."

"Relax."

"Hit down on the ball."

"Take the club straight back and straight through."

Those were the principles according to Brian and—to be fair—almost anybody to whom J.B. had spoken. J.B. had broken 90 a few times, but he mainly shot in the mid-90s, forever fighting that chronic slice.

J.B. and Brian were about as opposite as best friends could be, supporting the notion that opposites attract, even in friendships. J.B. was the good guy who normally did the right things; Brian was the rebel. J.B. added stability to Brian's life, and Brian added zest to J.B.'s. J.B. was a southerner who had grown up in Knoxville; Brian was a transplanted "yankee" from New York. The southern belles and down home country cookin' had swayed Brian to stay in Knoxville after graduating from U.T.

Although J.B. considered his friend the luckiest golfer he had ever seen, Brian had not been as lucky in love, having had an impulsive first marriage that failed. The marriage had produced a daughter, Melanie, the apple of Brian's eye, but he only got to see her when her mom came back from her new North Carolina home to visit relatives. Brian's motto was that he did what he wanted, when he wanted, and with whomever he wanted. However, he had remarried within a couple of years. His wife was expecting his second child. This had only mildly settled him down.

The Golden Tee Driving Range was on the south side of Knoxville, little more than a cow pasture with a fence to keep out cattle. There was a pretty equal split between grass areas and mats. There was a chipping, pitching and bunker area as well as an overly undulated putting green. It was hard to find a straight putt on this green, but it was good for working on breaking putts.

The pro shop had a few shirts and balls, and there were a couple of sets of clubs for sale, but dust had settled over all the merchandise, which had sat for years, undisturbed. One could buy a beer or a Coke and a variety of chips in the corner near the cash register. Billy Johnson, the assistant pro who worked there, was a top local player. He shot par on a regular basis, which was better than most golfers could imagine, and he did pretty well in local tournaments. A large bucket of balls was $5, even though some of the balls were past their prime. J.B. did the honors and bought two buckets for them to hit.

"How ya' feeling today?" Brian asked with a grin.

"Still a little numb from yesterday," J.B. declared.

"Grass or mats?" Brian asked.

"Definitely mats. I hit enough fat shots yesterday to last me till next year," J.B. declared.

"Well, we're gonna fix that today." Even with all the ribbing, gloating and wise-guy commentary Brian gave J.B., the fact remained that they were friends, and Brian really wanted to see his pal get better. Not so much better to deny himself a victory every weekend, but enough so J.B. would enjoy himself more on the golf course.

"How'd you like the game yesterday?" Brian quizzed.

"Another one in the win column," J.B. deadpanned.

"I'll tell you what, I was surprised when that tailback got up after the hit Al Wilson put on him in the third."

"To tell you the truth buddy, I don't remember much about it. I was still in a funk from the round yesterday."

Brian's eyebrows went up, and J.B. could see his friend's surprise. The revelation that he had been unable to pay attention to the Vols game put the seriousness of his mind set into a new perspective. The two friends walked all the way to the left end of the range and set down their clubs and extra-large buckets.

"All right, hit a couple of shots to warm up and we'll get started bringing you back from the dead," Brian commanded with his usual tone of confidence.

J.B. poured his balls into the flat basket that allowed the golfer to use his club to pull the next ball over to hit. He then began to make motions that would actually be hard to categorize as swings. A swing is a smooth back and forth motion. J.B.'s "swing" would be defined as whatever the dictionary labeled "quick, jerky, and discombobulated." Brian's "swings" could be categorized as less jerky, less quick and less discombobulated, but not by much.

Both men started with a seven-iron because they had read in an article that Ben Hogan recommended it. Without loosening up, they just got right to the business of hitting balls.

"Are you ready yet?" Brian asked, after they had hit about 10 shots each.

"Yeah, I guess."

"Okay. Let me see you hit a couple."

J.B. hit shots, and none of them suited him. His state of mind was so fragmented that frustration and disgust were all he could feel. He hit a thin shot that vibrated his fingers to the bone.

"Are you telling me you didn't look up on that one? Keep your head down and don't look up to watch the ball," Brian commanded. "I'll watch it for you."

"I'm not looking up," J.B. said, bitterness stiffening his lips. "I know I'm not. There is no way."

"Then what do you think it is, Mr. Hogan?" Brian quizzed sarcastically.

"I don't know what it is, but it isn't that. I've tried to keep my eye on the ball for all the years I've played golf, and it hasn't made me any better. If that were the answer, wouldn't I have gotten better?"

"Only if you had any ability in the first place," Brian said with a smile.

J.B. dismissed the obvious dig. "What if that's not the problem? What if I've been trying this for all these years and 'lifting my head' is not even the main problem?" J.B. demanded.

"It's one of the main fundamentals of golf. You know that."

"*Do* I know that? How do you know what the fundamentals are?"

"Just read any book or look at a magazine or video. They'll tell you," Brian vigorously defended.

"Ya know, there has to be more to being a good player than keeping my head down." Saturday's conversation with Rachel began to ring in his ears. "Brian, I'm going to get professional help," J.B. announced.

"What are you talking about?" Brian demanded.

"I'm talking about taking a lesson."

"You gotta be kidding me."

"No, I'm gonna sign up for one with the pro here, Jack. Jack Pierce."

"You know J.B., you *do* need professional help. The kind a psychologist can give you." Brian tried to talk some sense into his friend. "Look, every swing is different. It just takes some people longer than others to get better. Just watch any tournament. You can tell who's swinging just by their swing. They're all unique. Couples, Furyk, Trevino, Nicklaus, Woods. All different. I think you should learn it on your own. Some of the greatest players of all time were self-taught," Brian pointed out.

"I know, but how many self-taught players are like me, shooting 95 their whole life?"

"I don't know."

"I bet there's a lot. I've already decided. I'm gonna check with Jack today."

"Well, don't come crying to me the next time you're adding up another one-oh-five." The look on Brian's face showed that he was a little hurt to see J.B. forsaking his advice.

"No offense buddy, but I've gotta do this."

"Suit yourself," Brian replied, sighing with resignation.

Brian continued to hit balls as J.B. headed to the trailer that had been spruced up to serve as the pro shop. As he climbed the stairs, he noticed a sign that he had ignored in the past.

World-Renowned Instructor Jack Pierce
Available for Instruction by Appointment
$75 an Hour
Please see Jack or pro shop staff to sign up.

J.B. had watched Jack give lessons over in the far right corner of the range, which was reserved for his students. Jack had just retired from a job that had taken him away from the area in the early '80s. Before his departure, he had been known by some as the best teacher in Knoxville. He had been the teacher of a lot of the state's best players, as well as a former tour player, Jerry Damron. He was not here on this particular Sunday, so J.B. spoke to the assistant, Billy Johnson.

"Billy, how do I go about getting a lesson with Mr. Pierce?"

"You just have to tell me. I've got his book right here."

"What's available?"

"You name it."

"Let's try next Saturday at eight."

Billy scanned the page, finding that 8:00 was open. "That'll work."

"Is there anything I need to do before Saturday?" J.B. asked hesitantly.

"Nope. Jack likes you to come in with an open mind, because he's going to really bust your bubble on what you've thought about golf in the past."

"Is that good or bad?"

"You'll have to decide after your lesson. Personally, I like to keep it simpler than the way Jack does it."

"Are you saying that it's bad?"

"Nope. He's the expert. I'm a player. I don't know much about teaching."

"All right. Eight o'clock it is, for Saturday," J.B. declared.

"Okay. Have a good week, Mr. Hawkins."

J.B. returned to where Brian was finishing up his bucket. "Well, I took the plunge. I signed up for this coming Saturday."

"He's probably going to mess you up," Brian exclaimed with a roll of his eyes.

"I can't get any worse than I am now. Plus, I hear this guy is good."

"I'm telling you, you're making a mistake," Brian insisted.

"You're just worried that I'll start beating you." J.B. retorted, beaming.

"In your dreams!"

3
J.B.'s First Lesson

AFTER A WEEK OF THE USUAL WORK and household duties, Saturday arrived, a typical autumn day. J.B. wondered if he had done the right thing. *What if this guy does mess me up? Will he want to change everything?* Then he answered himself, *I don't have much to lose.* He got a couple of chores done while Rachel and the two little ones were just starting to rouse around on this lazy Saturday.

"Where are you off to today, honey?" Rachel asked.

"That golf lesson over at the Golden Tee. I thought I told you."

"I don't think so, since I'd have remembered winning an argument. But I'm glad you decided to do it. I know it wasn't an easy decision."

"No, it wasn't, but you were right. . . . I should have done this a long time ago," J.B. added.

"I'm sure it will help. What time is the lesson?" Rachel inquired.

"Eight o'clock."

"You'd better get going, or you'll be late."

"I know. I'm leavin'. I'll see you this afternoon."

"Hey, pick up some bread on your way home."

"All right." J.B. always forgot to pick up the bread.

As J.B. drove to the range, two thoughts filled his mind: excitement and fear. The excitement was prompted by the prospect of starting something new, multiplied by the possibility of finally getting better. The other thought was fear. *What if Brian's right? What if the answer is just more practice on my own? Maybe there is no right or wrong way to learn about golf. This better not be a waste of my time and money,* J.B. thought as he made the turn that led to Golden Tee.

As he pulled into the range, he put away both thoughts. He got his clubs out of the trunk, put on his spiked shoes and headed toward the pro shop. Billy greeted him in his customary nonchalant way.

"Hello, Mr. Hawkins."

"Hey, Billy. Where do I go for my lesson?"

"All the way down to the right where you see the roped off area. Here's a bucket of balls to get you warmed up."

J.B. headed toward the designated lesson area. He set his golf bag down and grabbed his seven-iron. He pulled a ball over from the basket and began to warm up. There was still an aggravating tendency to mis-hit the ball, thin on one and then behind it (or fat) on the next. The thin shots would get reasonable results, but fat shots were disastrous on the golf course.

He stopped hitting the balls and looked around. It must be getting close to time for his lesson. Where was Jack? J.B. looked at his watch. It was 8:05, and Jack was nowhere to be found. Being late was not something for which J.B. had much tolerance. He always tried to be at least 15 minutes early. Just then he saw a car barrel into the gravel parking lot. J.B. recognized Jack from having seen him one night at the range. A large man in his sixties, he had a face that made an instant, lasting impression, something akin to a stone face, J.B. thought. The man had the look of someone who was constantly suffering from indigestion.

J.B. had heard that Jack was opinionated and harsh. His "my way or the highway" personality wasn't exactly what J.B. was looking for, but his reputation as a golf expert was what had brought J.B. to the lesson. Jack rode over to the lesson area in his golf cart with his red and white Wilson professional bag attached to the back. The words "Jack Pierce, PGA Professional" were prominently displayed on the front of the big bag.

"You must be J.B.," Jack said without an apology for being late.

"Yes sir," J.B. said, extending his hand.

Jack threw his cigarette on the ground to free his right hand to shake. J.B. was unimpressed and a little irritated by Jack's tardiness and rude introduction.

"Well, let's get started," Jack growled. "First of all, as you might have heard, I have a very definite way that I teach. Before we start, I want to make sure you're committed to the changes that are coming."

"Oh yeah, I'm ready to change. My game is pathetic. I'm ready to get better right now."

"Well what I teach are *the* fundamentals of golf," Jack stated emphatically. "If you do what I ask you to do, you will become the *best* player that you can be. Let me watch you hit a couple."

"What club?"

"Go ahead and grab a six-iron," Jack answered.

J.B. yanked his six-iron out of his bag and started to hit a few shots. With his nervousness over taking lessons, he sliced the balls even more than usual. None of the shots felt good.

"Okay, son, that's enough. Let me tell you what I see. Your grip is too weak, your posture is slouched, and you line up too far to the right. Then when you swing"—Jack demonstrated as he spoke—"you take the club too far inside on the backswing, you have a reverse pivot, you come over-the-top when you start down, you're flipping at the bottom, and you're off balance. Other than that, it looks okay," Jack said sarcastically. "We've got a lot to do to get your swing where it needs to be."

J.B. knew it was bad, but he had no idea that it was this bad. Demoralized, he felt like sinking into the ground.

"All right, let's go ahead and get you started the right way," Jack said as he grabbed a club out of his massive bag. "A good golf swing, like building a house, starts with a solid foundation. In golf, that foundation is your pre-swing, which is grip, aim and set-up." Jack gripped the club and set up to the ball.

J.B. struggled to concentrate on Jack's words. He was still reeling from the critique that Jack had just given him.

"To take a proper grip," Jack continued, "I want you to put the club in the fingers of your left hand with the butt of the club under your heel pad." He demonstrated as he spoke.

"Is this what you're talking about?" J.B. asked, showing him his grip.

"Not exactly, but that's close. Let's make sure that when the grip is completed you can see two knuckles of the left hand." He looked closely at J.B.'s grip some more. "Now take your right hand and shake my hand. This is the way I want it on the club, right on the side, not on the top or the bottom of the handle, but on the side."

"Is this right?" J.B. asked while displaying his grip for Jack. "It feels very uncomfortable."

"Of course it does," Jack said impatiently. "Anything new is going to feel uncomfortable." Jack surveyed J.B.'s grip again. "That's better. So, let's move on to alignment." Jack laid two shafts on the ground parallel to each other, though J.B. didn't know the purpose. "In golf, alignment is not easy, because we have to stand sideways to our target. In other sports, we get to face our target. This creates a problem in golf that takes a lot of practice to overcome."

"I've always tried to line my shoulders up to the target," J.B. said hesitantly.

"Well, nothing good is going to come from that. That's the worst thing you can do. You must line the clubface up to the target and then your body aims parallel to that. We will practice with these two shafts on the ground to fix that problem." Jack pointed to the shafts that he had laid down. "The right shaft is your target line, and the left shaft is your body alignment. Try it." J.B. got into his stance and looked out toward the target.

"This doesn't feel right. I feel like I'm aimed twenty yards left of that flag."

"That's normal. Your perception is fooling you. You'll get used to it," Jack said matter-of-factly. "The next thing is posture and stance. Let me have you set up to the ball again." J.B. got into his set-up. "Okay, this has to change, too. Get rid of the knee flex."

J.B. straightened his legs a little, which felt very foreign, and felt a stretch in his back.

"No. I mean get *rid* of the knee flex," Jack reiterated in a demanding tone.

J.B. straightened some more.

"No! I want your legs straight!"

"Isn't this too much?"

"No. What I'm showing you is the way all great players stand. Have you ever seen Sam Snead or Freddie Couples?"

"I have," J.B. said, struggling to recall images of those players. For all his effort, J.B. could not remember seeing their legs so straight.

"This stance gives you more clearance to swing your arms." Jack pointed out the distance between J.B.'s hands and legs when standing straight-legged. "Now that your foundation is world class, let's move on to the swing itself."

With Jack moving through his version of the fundamentals at such a brisk pace, J.B. felt a little dizzy and overwhelmed. He was stunned by the changes to his set-up and the tone that Jack was now using. Still, he was the professional, and J.B. had signed on because he wanted to get better.

"The next step is a one-piece takeaway," Jack said.

J.B. had read about a one-piece takeaway in a magazine article, so he felt that he had a glimmering of understanding on this step.

"Go ahead and set up to the ball," Jack commanded. "Now, the first move away from the ball is to move your hands, arms, club, upper spine and lower spine to your right post, which is another term for your right leg." Jack reeled off the instructions quickly.

"It feels like I'm swaying," J.B. said as his head moved so that he was looking straight down to his right shoe. His head had moved at least eight inches when he moved everything to his "right post."

"That's the way all the great players do it. I've given lessons for years and, believe me, this is the way to be successful. To be athletic and have an athletic swing, you must shift your weight to your right post. From there you simply turn to the top."

Although it felt outrageous to him, J.B. reluctantly accepted this statement. After all, Jack was the pro.

"Practice that a few times, and then we'll move on to the next fundamental," Jack barked.

As J.B. practiced this awkward move, he kept telling himself to be committed. Suddenly he felt Jack's hands on his shoulders, moving him back to the right post to reinforce the feeling.

"Let's move now to the next fundamental," Jack said after a few moments, "which is the change of direction back toward the ball. When the club changes directions, your hip turns to the left and the club drops parallel to the ground." Jack demonstrated the move.

"The club drops that much?"

"Have you ever seen pictures of Ben Hogan?" Jack demanded.

"Yes, I have, but I didn't notice the club looking like this."

"Well I suggest that you go and look again, because this is a move that all the great players make."

J.B. was uncomfortable with this seemingly exaggerated movement, but he told himself to trust the instructor. Jack must know what he's talking about. J.B. tried the new moves a few times, with Jack keeping up a running commentary as he urged his student through the new positions.

"More. You still need to drop the club more. . . . Turn your hip sooner."

J.B. tried to hit balls with this new stance and movement, but he got off no more than ten shots before Jack moved on.

"The last fundamental is swinging to a complete finish. You must turn your hips completely. Your right shoulder will be closer to the target than your left, and your body will be in line with your left post." Jack pointed to J.B.'s left leg. As J.B. swung to this finish, Jack grabbed his hips and gave them a twist.

"You're not turning enough. You must swing to a complete finish," Jack emphasized with little patience.

J.B. tried again and felt that he had turned enough.

"You're still not turning enough!" Jack growled, again grabbing and twisting J.B.'s hips.

"This is all very new to me, Jack. And I've gotta be honest, it feels terrible."

Jack's face turned red with anger. "J.B., the difference between the students who get it and those who don't is commitment. I don't have time to babysit you. You either want my help or you don't."

"Hey, I was just making a comment. I thought you would want to know how it felt to me." J.B. bristled.

"I don't care what it feels like now. Of course it feels bad. It's different." Jack briefly suspended his tirade and sighed. "This is not easy. It takes dedication and practice."

"I'm really trying to do what you showed me," J.B. insisted.

"It will take dedication on your part," Jack replied, "and practice and continued lessons."

J.B. was disoriented from all the changes. It felt so wrong and was much more extreme than he had imagined. He had thought taking a lesson would give him a couple of ideas that would fix the problem that had plagued him for years. J.B. had also hoped Jack might give him the elusive "secret."

J.B., like most amateurs, believed there was one piece of information that could magically turn his game around. But today's lesson had been a textbook full of new ideas. How could he do everything that Jack had told him? J.B. had not taken a lesson to be berated. The one thing he knew was that he wanted to be as good a player as he could be, and he knew Jack had helped some people become good players in the past.

"I want to see you the same time next Saturday," Jack asserted.

"Okay. I'll practice a lot between now and then."

"That's what I want to hear—a man who's committed to these important changes. My next lesson has arrived, so I'll see you next week."

J.B. moved a couple of spots down and continued to hit balls. As he practiced, he hit a couple that he considered to be good ones, but the shots were mostly bad. His new address position was so foreign, with no knee flex, that he felt as though his legs were wooden. The takeaway felt like such a big sway, he thought he was going to fall down. The change of direction made him feel as though he might hit himself with the club. The extra turn of the hips in the finish felt as though he were twisting into the ground, and he found it very hard to maintain his balance. Ball after ball showed little improvement. He wondered what he should be focusing on, because trying to do them all at once wasn't working. As he got to the last ball in his bucket, he wasn't sure he had made any progress. He felt nothing but confusion and a little disbelief at how wrong he must have been doing things all these years.

J.B. managed to practice twice during the week, and at the second practice he felt more out of whack and disoriented than at the first. Why was this so hard? Is it supposed to feel this bad? He looked forward to his next lesson, because he had a lot of questions for Jack.

Saturday started out with breakfast and rough housing with the kids. The breakfast was especially good, with sausage from Rachel's grandfather, Pa Joe, in West Tennessee. *It might not be good for you, but it sure does taste good,* J.B. thought.

"I'm off to my lesson."

"How's it going so far?" Rachel asked.

"I don't know. I'm not hitting it any better, and I'm not sure if this is normal. He's making so many changes in my swing that it's tough to remember them all."

"Did he tell you how long it was going to take before you start getting better?"

"Kinda. But I'd like to get a more definite answer this week."

"Don't forget the bread again this week," Rachel added with little confidence.

"Oh, yeah. Don't worry, I won't. See you this afternoon."

J.B. drove to Golden Tee, got his balls from Billy, and headed toward Jack's teaching area. Jack was there before J.B. this time.

"Well, I see you didn't quit on me!" Jack said. "Sometimes the fundamentals of golf scare people off, but I can tell you're a person who is determined. I like that. One of the biggest reasons golfers don't get better is a lack of persistence. There is a *best* way to hit a golf ball, and the way I teach is the best way to hit a golf ball consistently. The other ways you've seen or read about are not as fundamentally sound."

"I've practiced this week, but I haven't hit the ball any better."

"Well, of course you haven't hit it any better yet! This a long term project," Jack said unsympathetically. "Let's get to work."

J.B. proceeded to hit a half-dozen shots, none of them feeling good to him. "I told you I was hitting it bad," he commented.

"And I told you last time that it would take time and commitment." Jack showed his ire at the comment. "This is when a lot of people quit. If it was easy, everybody could do it."

J.B. could see that Jack was not in the mood to discuss anything.

"Let me see how far you've gotten," Jack suggested in a more civil tone.

J.B. set up in the uncomfortable straight-legged stance. His alignment felt a little bit better, as did the grip. He took a swing trying to remember the backswing, the transition and the finish, but wasn't sure if he did any of them right. The ball went out to the right after being hit with the very bottom of the club.

"I told you to get rid of that knee flex and move everything to your right post on your one-piece takeaway."

J.B. hit another shot with about the same result.

"You're not flattening out the club enough on the downswing. Flatten it out more this time," Jack said as he grabbed J.B.'s club and pulled it down even with his belt buckle and parallel to the ground.

J.B. tried again, mentally checking off the instructions: straight legs . . . one-piece takeaway to the right post . . . flatten it out more in the downswing . . . complete finish with hip turn. The ball went out to the right even more.

"That was better in the transition," Jack declared. "Where the ball goes isn't going to tell us anything for a while. You just have to trust my feedback. Hit one more. Same thing."

J.B. did it again. Same result. "Jack, I'm really confused. I'm not sure what to think about."

"Confused? You feel confused? J.B., I'm teaching you the most advanced information on playing golf that there is. Once again, if it was easy, everybody could do it. You're not one of those people who wants everything handed to you on a silver platter are you?"

"No. I just can't tell when I'm doing it right and when I'm doing it wrong."

"Hit some more. And as we practice this, you're going to get it," Jack assured him. The adjustments went on for the remainder of the lesson. J.B.'s confusion grew, but Jack's resolve didn't waiver. "We will get as much done as your commitment level will allow."

"All right," J.B. said with a growing uncertainty.

"I'll see you again next Saturday. Same time. Keep practicing. You're going to get it," Jack boomed.

The events of the morning had J.B. baffled. Was Jack's way the best way to go about improving his golf game? He kept telling himself to "be committed." He planned to stay committed to working on *the* fundamentals Jack had taught him. J.B. knew that all things worth achieving take time, and he was not a quitter. All his life he had risen to the challenges that presented themselves. The idea of not seeing this through, no matter how difficult it might be right now, was not a possibility.

After work on Tuesday, he went to the Golden Tee to practice. The new stance and movements felt more comfortable than before, but that wasn't saying much. J.B. noticed that Jim Ferguson was practicing a couple of spots down from him. He and J.B. had been acquaintances since being teamed up in a charity tournament a couple of years earlier. Jim taught at the high school and was the coach of their very successful baseball program. He was a single-digit handicap golfer who was always in the hunt at his club championship. He seemed to know quite a bit about the swing, though J.B. didn't know how he had learned. J.B. had wanted to ask him for advice on other occasions, but Jim was very focused when he practiced. J.B. didn't want to bother him. On this night, Jim noticed J.B. practicing and turned to say hello.

"Hey J.B., how are ya? Are you changing your swing? It looks . . . different." Jim seemed to pause on the word *different*, as though he were searching for the most diplomatic word for the situation.

"Yeah, I've been taking lessons from Jack Pierce, and he's changing everything."

"From Jack, huh? I don't know about Jack's *fundamentals*. They certainly are different than the ones I was taught. And they're different than the ones he used to teach, back before he left Knoxville for his corporate job in the early eighties."

"Well, I'm going to stick with it. I want to give this enough time to work."

"Hey, I respect that. It's just that . . . well, when you swing, by the time you finish it looks like you're going three different directions and then get twisted like a pretzel." Jim demonstrated as he spoke.

"It feels like that, too, but I've gotta give it a chance."

"If it doesn't work out, come and talk to me. I have some advice for you."

"Go ahead and tell me. I'll take all the advice I can get."

"No. I'll wait and see how your lessons work out with Jack."

"Okay. I know where you're coming from, Jim. We'll have to go play sometime . . . if you can handle playing with a hacker."

"Yeah, we'll do it. Just call me at school." He turned and walked over to the putting green.

J.B. didn't know what Jim meant by "I have some advice for you," but he needed to finish up and get home. *It was nice of him to take the time to comment on my efforts*, J.B. thought.

Jim had confirmed to J.B. that his swing looked to others the way it felt to him. He finished his bucket and left.

On the drive home, J.B. realized that he was becoming obsessed with this. He thought about his golf swing all the time, talked about it at lunch, and scribbled reminders to himself about his backswing. Deep in thought, he arrived home without the bread. He would practice again on Thursday and, perhaps, would see some progress.

* * *

The only lighted range on the south side of town, the Golden Tee was packed on Thursday evenings with people wanting to practice for their Saturday round. Brian had called J.B. to let him know he was coming out to hit some balls. They hadn't seen each other or played since their Sunday session three weeks earlier. J.B. could already hear what Brian was going to say. Since he arrived first, J.B. went down to the left to find a couple of open spots.

The Golden Tee used a back row of mats to let the grass recover, but these spots were on the grass area. Practicing next to them was Sam Mathis, who had played for the Vols golf team during J.B. and Brian's years there. They had met playing pick-up basketball. Sam had taken lessons from Jack as a junior player in the '70s, and most people said he would have made the tour if he had only had the head for it . . . and putted better.

"Hey, Sam! How're ya doing? What are you doing practicing here? I've never seen you out here."

"I've moved, so this is close for me now, and it's the only lighted range around," Sam said in between swings.

"How are you hitting it these days?" J.B. asked.

"I'm hitting it good. I just need to putt better. What else is new?" Sam pondered his own question for a split second before focussing his attention on J.B. "I didn't know you played golf."

"I took it up when I was at UT, but I've only been serious the last couple of years. I've started taking lessons with Jack Pierce the last couple of weeks."

"How's he doing? I haven't seen him since he got back."

"He's doing pretty well. He teaches down on the other end of the range." J.B. pointed.

"I'll have to come see him sometime," Sam said, while looking back toward his range balls. "We'd better get to practicing before the range closes on us."

J.B. started to warm up and Sam continued where he had left off. Sam's swing was a thing of beauty. It reminded J.B. a lot of Payne Stewart's swing, which was high praise indeed. If this swing developed from working with Jack, he knew he was doing the right thing. Brian finally showed up and took his spot between J.B. and Sam.

"Well, it's about time," J.B. mockingly scolded.

"That traffic is really getting bad. How's it been going? I haven't heard from you in awhile."

"I know. I've been busy with work and projects at home, and I've been working hard on my swing."

"Oh yeah, how's that going?" Brian asked cynically.

"It's hard to tell so far, but I'm going to keep working on it."

"Okay. Let's see it," Brian said as he turned to watch J.B.'s new swing. The first few weren't very good, but J.B. was trying the moves that he and Jack had worked on. Sam turned to watch.

"Are you sure Jack told you to swing like that?" Sam asked. "That's a whole lot different than what he used to show me. He didn't have me standing with my legs straight, and I sure didn't have all those loops." He moved over to show J.B. the positions that Jack used to have him practice.

"Yeah, buddy," Brian chimed in. "I don't know how that feels, but it's painful to watch. Are you sure that's what you're supposed to do?"

As J.B. was about to respond, a voice boomed from behind him. "Don't listen to those guys! They don't know what they're talking about." Jack was stalking toward them, his eyes as wide as saucers, his face red. Before J.B. could say a word, Jack was pointing his finger at J.B.'s nose. "And another thing, I don't teach quitters." His voice raised to a crescendo. "If you want to quit, you can quit *right now*." He turned on his heel and marched away.

J.B. was stunned. Brian and Sam were shocked. The patrons within earshot had stopped to see what was going on, so it was total embarrassment and humiliation for J.B. The outburst had come out of nowhere. Under normal circumstances, J.B. would have gone after Jack and straightened this out, but the scene was so bizarre that he was frozen in silence.

"What was that all about?" Brian asked.

"I have no idea," J.B. said, still stunned.

"He didn't even recognize me," Sam interjected. "I can tell you this, J.B., Jack has lost it. I think he's gone over the edge. The swings you were making were not his old fundamentals. He must be trying out something new on you. And Jack was always pretty tough, but he would never embarrass anybody the way he just did."

"Yeah, this decision to take lessons just keeps getting better and better," Brian said.

"Well, if this is the way lessons work, who needs 'em?" J.B. pulled over another ball and angrily hit it into the range. After a couple more shots, his anger boiled over. "I can't believe that guy. If all teachers are like Jack, why would anyone take a lesson? Professional golf instructor, yeah, right. I paid good money for humiliation and confusion, and I'm pretty sure I've done permanent damage to my lower back. I'll go back to figuring it out on my own."

"I hate to tell you that I told you so, but . . . I told you so," Brian said.

"Shut up!" J.B. had had enough of Brian's lip.

J.B. swore off lessons and golf instructors. He had given it a try, expecting to get a lot better and learn something. Instead he learned how to contort himself into a swing which was not only physically tough on him but, as Brian said, it was also ugly to watch. He continued to make the same mistakes, and he got the same quick tips from his friends and the golf magazines. The patented banana slice and scores of 93, 97 and 95 were not going away.

4

You're NOT Lifting Your Head!

"HEY, UMP! DO I NEED TO BRING YOU MY GLASSES?" Joey Thompson's dad yelled from the three-level bleachers that were no more than 30 feet from the third base line. J.B. pretended not to hear him as he yelled encouragement from the dugout to the little baseball players with "Fred's Hardware" stitched onto their shirts. J.B.'s main goals as a coach were keeping the eight-year-olds from getting hurt, convincing the outfielders to go down on one knee to catch a grounder, and ensuring that the kids had fun and wanted to keep playing the game. His own Little League experience as a boy hadn't been a good one, with yelling parents, screaming coaches and bad sportsmanship all around. After he reluctantly allowed himself to be talked into being the assistant coach, he decided to make sure the kids on his team had a better time.

"Play hard, do your best, and have fun" was the motto he preached. Nick, in third grade, now, loved it, and he was having so much fun. He used his Dad's old glove, not knowing that a new one was coming for his next birthday. They spent many hours playing catch in their new back yard.

In between baseball practices, games and his job, J.B. was hard at work on their new house. It fit most of Rachel's wants and all three of J.B.'s: a Jacuzzi bath, a swimming pool and a roof that didn't leak. Purchased in the spring, it was an antebellum home they got for a real bargain. With a few touch-ups and a fresh coat of paint, it had become a treasure to the family. It was quite a change from the little house on Maple Street. Brian was often recruited to help out with the renovations, and he always offered plenty of tips and suggestions on how to do everything better. J.B. thought Brian might have watched *This Old House* a few too many times.

Afternoons at home were often filled with the plunking of Margaret's melodies on the new piano. When they bought the house, the piano was purchased as a present for her sixth birthday. Margaret was also presented with a set of lessons from one of Knoxville's finest teachers. Mrs. Applewhite had come highly recommended. So far, Margaret seemed to respond well to the lessons, even though the experienced teacher had misgivings about beginning lessons for a child before age seven. The size of Margaret's hands kept her from spanning an octave, but the teacher took things slowly, ensuring that the student had grasped the fundamentals before moving ahead. She created a real appreciation for music in her students.

A year and a half had passed since J.B.'s ill-fated lessons with Jack Pierce, and his interest in golf was at an all time low. He hadn't completely quit golf, but he was close. To play for so long with little improvement was hard to take. There were too many fun things to do in the four hours it took to play a round of golf.

However, spring was a time of renewal, and a ritual that had started for J.B. in 1986 was about to come around again—watching the Masters. The Masters was the true signal of a new golf season. Not only was Augusta National beautiful, with its blooming dogwoods and azaleas, it had consistently created great drama on the back nine of the Sunday final round. How vividly J.B. could remember the 1986 Masters during his freshman year in college. Jack Nicklaus, the Golden Bear, making one dramatic shot after another on his way to a back nine 30 and his sixth Masters title at the age of 46. In retrospect, it seemed like fate. Everything that needed to happen that day to allow Jack the victory, did. Steve Ballesteros pulled his second shot into the water on the par five fifteenth. Tom Kite missed a lot of makeable birdie putts. And Greg Norman made birdies on thirteen through seventeen to pull even with Nicklaus, only to push his second shot on eighteen into the crowd and make bogie. Little did anyone know the inexplicable defeats in majors that would befall "The Shark" in the coming years.

J.B. had gone to Brian's apartment, and they were yelling at the TV screen as Nicklaus made his dramatic birdie on sixteen and Steve pulled his ball into the water on the fifteenth. J.B. told Brian that day that he wanted to be taken to play as soon as possible. The visions of playing a great game well and at some point having a round like the Golden Bear's filled him with the promise of his new endeavor.

Each year after that, he had made a point to watch the Masters, an activity that energized him for the new golf season. He and Brian actually made the trek from Knoxville to Augusta for the practice rounds and par three tournament until the number of practice round tickets were limited. He could appreciate the telecast even more after seeing how far the 485-yard tenth hole drops off down the hill. The television cameras just don't do justice to the elevation changes and the undulations in the greens. The front nine, which is rarely seen on the telecast, surprised J.B. with its difficulty. A friend had told him he would place him on all eighteen greens in regulation, and he'd bet that J.B. couldn't break 80. After seeing the course, J.B. believed it. The slope and speed of the greens was unlike anything he had seen. He followed most of the great players at these practice rounds over the years, but Jack Nicklaus had remained his favorite.

The 1999 Masters was another great one, with story lines abounding. Three of them were Norman, Love and Olazabal. Greg Norman's talented play and excruciating losses had made him a crowd favorite, and he was in the hunt again. Davis Love III was a local favorite for two reasons, for his residence in not-to-distant Sea Island, Georgia, and for his desire to win one for his dad. Jose Maria Olazabal had been told that he might never walk again, much less play golf.

When Olazabal won the tournament, J.B. was inspired, thinking, *I can't give up, either. I'll have to find a way to conquer this game.* As he followed the play and carefully scrutinized some of the swings, he felt the desire to go to the range. The urge to practice hadn't hit him in more than a year. Now it was, surely, spring again, for he had newfound hope for the coming season.

"I'm going to hit some balls after work today over at Ironwood. I'll be home by eight," he said as he was leaving the house one morning the following week.

"Sure! I'll see you about nine," Rachel said knowingly.

"Yeah, you're probably right," J.B. said, laughing. "You need me to pick up anything?"

She rolled her eyes, knowing better than to respond.

"Okay. I'll see you tonight." He left her with a peck on the cheek.

When he got to the range he saw a familiar face. "Hey, what's the latest?" Jim Ferguson's voice carried out above the sounds of clubs hitting golf balls. "I haven't seen you in a while. What have you been up to?"

"Ahh, the same old thing. I've just been hacking it around. There's not much to tell."

"The last time I saw you, you were taking lessons with Jack Pierce, and I thought we were going to play sometime. That was almost two years ago!"

"Well, I'm sorry about that. I sort of had a bad experience with Jack. I swore off lessons after that deal. It was right after I saw you that I had a run-in with him over at Golden Tee."

"Well, you should've come to see me," Jim said seriously. "I told you I had some advice that would help you, and now I feel bad that you've wasted all this time trying to figure it out yourself."

"Hey, I haven't seen you. Besides, I wasn't looking for anymore instruction."

"The advice I was going to give you then, is the same advice I'm going to give you now. I know a truly great teacher here in Knoxville, and I want you to go see him. He will change your mind about golf instructors and what a teacher should be."

"I don't know, Jim. Jack was supposed to be the best teacher in Knoxville. I think I'd rather be a hacker than go through that again."

"What happened?"

"He told me to do this," J.B. said as he started to demonstrate the disjointed moves that he had been taught.

"I remember. That's what you were doing at the driving range the last time I saw you. Let me guess. He showed you all of that in one lesson."

"That's right."

Jim was shaking his head. "You know I coach the baseball team at Farragut High, and I want you to imagine me trying to teach my players all the fundamentals of hitting a baseball in one session. It would be ridiculous. We lose our common sense when we get to golf."

"I hadn't thought of it that way."

"Once I decide on my players after the tryout, I have my team come to practice five days a week. And guess what we work on?"

"The fundamentals."

"That's right. Throwing, catching, running, hitting and bunting every day. I break it up and build habits. Good habits hold up under pressure. It's the basic idea of teaching any motor skill. You break up the skills into smaller units, and you build from simple to complex."

"And this guy teaches golf that way?"

"He sure does. He teaches you the way golf should be taught. He calls it uncommon sense, because in golf, common sense is so uncommon. He actually named his golf instruction business UnCommon Golf. And get this . . . he has a money-back guarantee policy."

"A money-back guarantee? I've never heard of a pro doing that. Tell me, though, what makes him so good?"

"You'll have to meet him to find out. His name is Harry Wilkinson, but his students call him 'Coach.' He's over at Fox Run Country Club. I'll give you his phone number, and I'm not taking no for an answer. You call him!"

"Harry Wilkinson, huh? The 'Coach.' I guess I've got nothing to lose. I can always get my money back."

"I can assure you that you won't ask for your money back."

The thought of more lessons did not appeal to J.B., but if he didn't really have to risk anything, he had nothing to lose. He still wanted to play golf a lot better and start beating Brian.

"Okay, Jim. Where's that phone number?"

"Do you have a pen?"

J.B. pulled a pen out of his pocket and handed it to Jim, who found an old scorecard and scribbled the number.

"Here you go. In fact, I'm going to be checking to make sure you call him," Jim said.

"Hey, thanks. I'll let you know how it goes. We still need to get together and play."

"Just let me get through baseball season and then we will."

"Sounds like a plan."

The next day J.B. called the number.

"Fox Run Country Club golf shop. How can I help you today?"

"Yes, my name is J.B. Hawkins, and I'd like to set up a lesson with Harry Wilkinson."

"I have Coach Wilkinson's book right here. Did you know he's booked for at least a month, sir?"

"No, I didn't know that. When's the first available lesson?"

"Let's see . . . the first available is May 15, which is a Saturday. You can choose either a six-lesson package, a ten-lesson package or his year-long program."

"I'd really just like one, but I guess I have to go with the six. He's got the money-back guarantee, right?"

"Yes, he does. If you are not completely satisfied after the first lesson, he will give you your money back."

"Okay, then. Sign me up for a six-lesson package," J.B. said reluctantly. He was still cautious after his lessons with Jack and wanted to check Harry out.

"I've got you at eleven o'clock on Saturday, May 15, Mr. Hawkins. Harry also has a clinic every week that is very popular, and it's free. He does that at one o'clock every Saturday."

"That sounds good. I'll have to come see that before my lesson."

"Have a great day, Mr. Hawkins. You're going to learn a lot from Harry."

Even the beginning seemed better this time around, and J.B. liked the fact that Harry came so highly recommended. Being booked a month in advance was certainly a sign that this guy was good. J.B. was definitely going to a Saturday clinic to see what this Harry Wilkinson character was all about.

The following Saturday, J.B. went to Fox Run for the clinic. He had convinced Brian to come along and skip playing golf for a week. Fox Run was a very nice, semi-private club. They had a strong membership, and the course was known for being in good shape all the time. The shop staff was professional and pleasant as they directed J.B. and Brian out to the range. When they got there, they were surprised. About 200 people were there, ranging in age from eighth graders to retirees who had come to see and hear "Coach," and since there were only about 50 chairs, for most it was standing room only.

The chairs were set up in a backward L, and in the area in front of the chairs, balls were teed up like rows of soldiers in formation. The chairs at the bottom of the L looked over the balls toward the range, which was a practice paradise. There were bunkers surrounding target greens, and the turf for hitting balls was like carpet. J.B. and Brian saw Harry warming up as he spoke to the people around him. He was of medium build with graying hair that stuck out around the edge of his straw hat. The coach was in good physical condition, which showed in his distinguished and athletic swing. Everything looked effortless as he hit a few more warm-up shots.

Harry rested his club on his shoulder and raised his voice for the crowd. "I'd like to welcome everyone out to beautiful Fox Run Country Club and to my weekly clinic, "How to Turn Your Game Around." For those who don't know me, I'm Harry Wilkinson. I am committed to entertaining you and turning your game around through proper instruction."

He flashed a dazzling smile. "You all can absolutely be better golfers, and I will convince you of that fact over the next hour. The first half of the clinic will be today's topic, 'No More Slicing,' as advertised. The second part is a question and answer session. So be thinking of questions you'd like to ask me."

Harry gazed around the audience. "Without any further ado, let's get started. Today we are talking about the slice. How many here slice it?"

A majority of the audience raised their hands; most were only halfway up, like half-salutes beside sheepish grins. J.B. pictured his ball curving from left to right as he raised his hand.

"That answer has been common ever since I've been teaching. But I can tell you this: *nobody* that I teach still slices.

You do not have to keep slicing. Let me show you where it comes from and what to do about it." Harry had everyone's attention as he continued. "Because most people start out without proper instruction, they do not get a proper grip. The grip controls the clubface. If the clubface is pointed in the same direction as the path at impact, there is no sidespin."

At this point Harry began to demonstrate. He used a magnetic pointer on his clubface to show the clubface angles. He then started to hit the balls that were in perfect rows. He was a master showman, exaggerating each point and getting lots of laughs along the way. He hit shot after shot to get his point across. He showed how an out-to-in path with the face pointed to the right leads to the slicing sidespin. Within 20 minutes he had hit most of the teed up balls in a series of demonstrations.

"You don't have chronic slicers in tennis, because tennis players pay attention to that big racket face. They point it left for a cross-court forehand and square it up for down the line shots. The face is so much smaller in golf that players don't pay attention to it."

He demonstrated the face pointing to the left and how the ball would go left. He then demonstrated the face being square to the path and how the ball would go to wherever the path was going. He continued to demonstrate and explain, and as his first half of the clinic came to a conclusion he said, "Anyone here who gets proper instruction, which should also be fun, will get rid of their slice forevermore. And let me say it one more time: no more slicing. Thank you."

The 30 minutes had passed quickly. He received hearty applause from the group and then opened the clinic for questions.

"Yes." Harry pointed to a lady on his left with a raised hand.

"I top the ball a lot, and my husband says that I'm lifting my head, even though I know I'm staring at the golf ball."

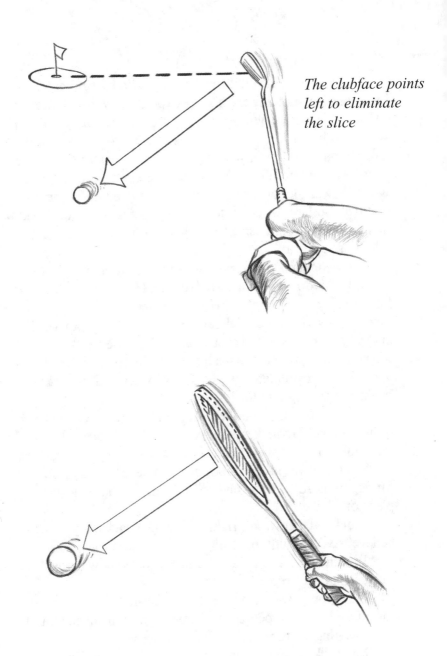

The clubface points left to eliminate the slice

"You don't have chronic slicers in tennis, because tennis players pay attention to that big racket face."

"I'm glad you brought that up." Harry's energy seemed to jump another notch, and his eyes sparkled with enthusiasm. "That is one of my favorite subjects. As a matter of fact, that is what my clinic is on next week. It's called 'You're *Not* Lifting Your Head,' and I want you to get anybody that you have ever heard say they're lifting their head to come to the clinic next week. It will totally change how you think about striking the golf ball. So I'm not going to completely answer that question until next week, but I can tell you this: you're . . . not . . . lifting . . . your . . . head."

Harry continued to answer questions, putting on a fantastic show. He hit drives with a 60-inch driver. He hit drives while on his knees and from a chair. He hit tee shots with a putter and made many other demonstrations to prove his points. The audience was still somewhat stunned by his statement about not lifting the head, which was the buzz after the clinic ended. Harry was then surrounded by people who wanted to ask him questions and sign up for lessons.

"No wonder he's booked a month in advance. That was quite a clinic! He makes you *want* to take lessons," J.B. said with only a hint of skepticism.

"Yeah, he was pretty good, but he's dead wrong about not lifting the head," Brian said, still defending his longstanding piece of advice.

"I told you that wasn't right a long time ago, but you didn't believe me." J.B. got in his dig.

"I'll definitely be here next Saturday to see how he explains this," Brian declared.

The group was starting to diminish with Harry still surrounded by a few people. J.B. went up to introduce himself. After waiting his turn, he met his new teacher.

"Mr. Wilkinson, my name is J.B. Hawkins, and I've signed up with you for a six-lesson package."

"J.B., call me Harry or Coach, not Mr. Wilkinson. I'm sorry about the month wait, but if you come to the clinics you will understand a lot before your lessons." Harry's voice glowed with enthusiasm. His larger-than-life personality made J.B. think everyone who met him must feel that they were in the presence of greatness.

"You certainly got everyone's attention about slicing and not lifting the head. I'm really interested to hear about that next week. I'm going to come with this skeptical one next to me," he said, pointing to Brian.

"I understand the skepticism, and I'll show you what really happens next week. Guys, I have to get to my two-thirty lesson. Thanks for introducing yourselves."

At the far-end of the double-ended range was Harry's studio, a neat, stylish building that matched the style of the clubhouse. He drove down in his cart to make his 2:30 lesson.

"I'm going to set up a tee-time for next Saturday in the morning, so that you, Robby, Bill and I can come to the clinic," J.B. proposed.

"That sounds good. Robby and I need some more of the money we get from you guys," Brian replied.

"We'll see about that."

The clinic had rekindled J.B.'s desire to be a better player. The wall of distrust that had been put up after Jack's lessons was starting to come down. Coach seemed to be everything Jack wasn't, Harry was entertaining and understandable, and he showed a concern for the improvement and enjoyment of golfers. After his explanation in the clinic, J.B. could picture himself hitting the ball straight instead of that weak, pitiful slice that had plagued him throughout his golf-playing career so far. Harry's next clinic would certainly explain why he didn't hit the ball solidly. He could imagine how much more fun it would be to play golf and have an idea of what he was doing instead of being confused most of the time. He could just picture beating Brian and wiping that smug grin off of his face.

Robby Blackwell and Bill Brownson completed their usual Saturday foursome. Robby worked as the sales manager for his uncle's Ford dealership and did very well. Brian had bought his last three cars from Robby, and a decent friendship had developed. He was a good guy, a little loud for J.B.'s taste, but a good guy just the same. He and Brian would team up against J.B. and Bill, who was everyone's insurance agent. Although he was pretty successful in his field, self-confidence was not exactly his strong suit, especially when it came to golf. J.B. called Bill and Robby about playing and going to the clinic to hear, once and for all, why they topped the ball.

On Saturday they all showed up 40 minutes early for their 8:00 tee time. It was another beautiful day. The weather had been spectacular this spring, adding to the high they had been on since their beloved Vols had won the National Championship in January. They bought two buckets of balls to split among them and held off on the usual banter until they arrived on the first tee.

"Okay gentlemen, same as usual?" Brian asked on the first tee.

"You've got it. Two dollar Nassau for the team, and you and I have our same individual bet," J.B. answered. "Hey, Bill, you ready to take it to these guys today?"

"I hope I can do something right today," Bill said.

"We're going to let you guys have the honors on the first hole, since you won't have them the rest of the day." Robby chimed in on the banter. Everyone hit their tee shots to begin the round. J.B. had never beaten Brian, and this day was no exception. J.B. tried some things that Harry had talked about in his clinic, especially the part about not slicing. He tried to get the clubface to point to the left at impact, and when he managed to do that, it didn't slice . . . it went straight left, out of bounds. After this experiment didn't work, he played his normal way and shot a 93. Brian shot an 85 and won their match going away. Brian and Robby also won the team match on all three bets, and they let J.B. and Bill hear about it as they ate lunch at the club.

"I've gotta be honest, guys," Robby said, chuckling. "Most

people would have gotten sick and tired of getting beat all the time and probably given up. But you two keep coming back for more. I'm impressed."

"Yeah, J.B. You better hope these lessons kick in soon, or you'll be able to claim me on your tax return as a dependent," Brian said as he nudged Robby.

"Your winning days are numbered," J.B. countered, bringing his club sandwich up for another bite. "You better gloat while you can."

"Sorry I let you down partner," said Bill, who never quite played to his 18-handicap. "I was dead weight out there today."

"No problem, Bill. We'll get 'em soon enough."

Upon finishing lunch, J.B. led the group over to the range in time to catch the clinic that might do the impossible: get Brian to be quiet for more than five minutes.

When they got to the range, they could not believe their eyes. The crowd for this clinic was double the number for the previous week. Obviously, a few people had spread the word. The balls were once again set up in their perfect rows, and there were more chairs set out than there had been a week earlier. Harry was warming up, hitting each ball with the same amount of curve, which was impressive to the assembled group. The time had come, and Harry started the clinic.

"Welcome, welcome, welcome. I'm delighted by the turnout and know that you are ready for today's topic: 'You're *Not* Lifting Your Head.' Let me get started by saying that I understand why this misconception has gone on for so long. I respect all of you for coming here today and for your love of the great game of golf. I'm not going to say anything to embarrass anyone. When you understand what I'm telling you, with some work, you can become a very good ball striker."

Coach paused for an instant, then began. "How many of you have ever been told after topping a shot, 'You lifted your head'?"

The majority raised their hands.

"I know most people have been told this after topping it, and I know that some of you have even said it yourself. I have to tell you that in all my years of teaching, I have never seen a player lift his head through impact and mis-hit a shot."

There was a murmur in the audience. This was an astonishing statement to most who were there.

"Over the years, I have challenged anyone to bring this to me on videotape. To date it hasn't happened, and it won't happen. What is really happening? I'm sure you're wondering. Well, I'm glad you asked."

He smiled as a wave of laughter moved through the crowd.

"When I was a young teacher, which was years ago, I used to think people were raising or lifting their head. During a lesson, I would actually tell a student to keep his or her head down. But then I began to watch film in slow motion. I noticed these golfers, if they did anything, kept their head down way past impact. The thing I could not see with my naked eye was what I began to call scooping, the ill-fated attempt to help the ball into the air. It is this desire to lift the ball into the air that leads to the weight staying on the back foot and the wrists flipping upward." He demonstrated this movement as he described it.

"This, in turn, either results in hitting behind the ball or catching it on the way up, which is the topped shot. Because it happens so fast and people do eventually look up to see the ball, golfers for years have diagnosed it as lifting the head. Let me tell you why this distinction is so important. If you think you are lifting your head, then the cure is to keep your head down . . .

"It is this desire to lift the ball into the air that leads to the weight staying on the back foot and the wrists flipping upward."

which, unfortunately, doesn't cure the scooping problem. If you understand that the loft of the club gets the ball into the air"—he used his pointer club to show loft—"then you will realize it is your job to learn how to hit the ball solidly and let the loft get the ball into the air. Proper impact position is when the weight is on the left side and the handle of the club is leaning slightly forward. This is what allows you to hit the ball solidly."

Harry started to demonstrate scoop shots, and it was hilarious to the audience to see him emulate the movements they had all witnessed golfers do for years. Each time he demonstrated, he either topped the ball or hit behind it. He also kept moving his head lower and lower and still topped it. He then demonstrated proper impact position. The ball made that beautiful, distinctive sound one hears on the driving range of any tour event. He exaggerated the proper impact position and hit the ball lower and lower. He also did it in slow motion so everyone could see it.

J.B. wasn't sure about anyone else, but it made all the sense in the world to him. He somehow had known he wasn't lifting his head, but he had never had it explained as clearly and beautifully as Harry had just done.

Harry got serious for a moment. "I would like to make a plea to you, as I always do in these clinics. I am on a crusade to get serious golfers to find a qualified instructor and learn golf correctly. It is a great game that you can enjoy for a lifetime. And you can enjoy it even more when you are improving. Michael Jordan had a coach and so did Jack Nicklaus. If they needed coaches, don't you think it could help you?"

The majority of heads were nodding.

"Typically, golfers spend three hundred to one thousand dollars on clubs. You should be willing to spend a similar amount on learning how to use them. My assistant, Lenny, and

"Proper impact position is when the weight is on the left side and the handle of the club is leaning slightly forward."

I would love to show you how to play golf to your fullest potential. It will be both a rewarding and satisfying experience."

Harry paused and looked at each of those who had come out for the clinic. "Now, on with the show. Let's open it up for questions." He gazed at the many hands that went up. "Yes, what is your question?" He called on one of the men in the back row.

"I'm not convinced. I can't believe I have never heard this until now. How did 'keep your head down' become so common, if it weren't true?"

"That's a great question!" Harry's enthusiasm was at a fever pitch. "As you can see, this topic really charges me up. Most of golf's so-called fundamentals like 'head down,' 'left arm straight' and 'straight back straight through' have some truth to them. But the problem is they are over-simplified and have become misconceptions rather than correct concepts. I use these as the topics for my clinics because I want to change the way you perceive golf. Keeping your eye on the ball is not wrong, but it does not automatically get you to hit the ball solidly. You can very easily scoop while keeping your head down."

Harry demonstrated with his usual flair. The wrist obviously flipped while his eyes were just as obviously glued to the ball. The ball bounced and then rolled slowly off the front of the tee.

"So, keeping the eye on the ball is not the cure. Blind golfers can play golf because they learn to feel where the bottom of their swing is and where their ball is. I can close my eyes and hit good shots." Again Harry demonstrated masterfully. "I hope that answers your question, and I would be glad to discuss this with you afterwards. Next question." Coach pointed to a woman to his right, in the second row.

"Harry, my husband has told me to keep my head down for years. How am I going to tell him he's wrong?"

The audience erupted in laughter.

"Verrry carefully," Harry said, laughing, having known this question was coming. "I would suggest that you bring him when I do this topic again next month. It's usually easier to take from a third party. Make sure to bring him next time." Harry pointed to another hand. "Yes sir, what is your question?"

This continued with Harry answering any questions his opening subject had created. J.B. could tell that light bulbs were going on in the minds of the audience as they became convinced that Harry was right and that this information could change their game. J.B. knew that most were considering taking lessons with Harry or his assistant, Lenny Griffin, who was making a name for himself and giving lessons to those who could not get on Harry's overloaded lesson book.

For a change, Brian didn't have much to say. In fact, no one could say anything because they had all, at least, thought they or someone else was "lifting his head." As Harry was about to finish, he was challenged.

"I know I lift my head," a man in the back row blurted out.

"Okay. Stay after, and I'll get you on videotape," Harry said, showing no signs of irritation with the challenge. It was apparent that he had expected to be challenged. He again addressed the entire crowd. "Thank you for coming today. Tell your friends to come and learn about this great game of golf, to enhance their enjoyment."

Many stayed after the clinic to introduce themselves to Harry and to see the video of Harry's challenger. J.B.'s foursome stood by, watching Harry videotape as the man swung.

"On which swings did you lift your head?" he asked. "I want to play it back in slow motion."

As the video was put into slow motion for review, they saw that, sure enough, the wrists were bent, the weight stayed back on his right foot and his head stayed down well past impact. The man was, clearly, astonished.

"That's hard for me to believe. I just knew I was the exception to what you were saying."

Harry consoled the man. "That's a normal reaction. I'll change this misconception one person at a time, if I have to. I know this piece of information will help your game, and I wish you the best of luck. If you want to get a lot better, we would feel honored to help you."

The man shook Harry's hand and told him he would be signing up for lessons.

Harry recognized J.B. and said, "I'm glad to see you back."

"Great clinic today," J.B. declared.

"Thank you. I'm glad you enjoyed it," Harry replied.

"Harry, I have to be honest with you. I had a bad lesson experience. And even though everything you say makes sense, I'm still gun shy about lessons. So I have a request. Would it be possible for me to come watch you teach for a day?"

Harry thought for a second. His hesitance could be seen on his face as he rubbed his chin. "I normally don't allow that, because of the possibility of my student's being uncomfortable with it. But I'll do it this time on the condition that you make no comments to my students as you watch."

J.B. agreed, and they decided on the upcoming Saturday. The 2:30 lesson was once again the reason Harry had to depart. He thanked the remaining group for coming and headed toward his studio.

"What a class act! Man, he makes you believe you can learn golf, and his information makes more sense than anything I've heard before," J.B. said emphatically.

"It was a good show, but I don't know if I buy it yet," Brian said.

"What's there not to buy? It's obvious. Keeping the head down hasn't made me a better golfer. And Harry's ideas make sense."

"You're just desperate to believe it. If keeping the head down through impact was wrong, we would have heard about it by now, don't you think?" Brian said, defending his logic.

"Brian, were we at the same clinic? He was showing how topping the ball and hitting behind it are caused by scooping, not by picking the head up. I'm going to videotape you and see what you look like at impact."

"I don't need to see my swing on video," Brian responded with little enthusiasm.

Robby and Bill had both seemed to enjoy Harry's show, and both were grinning at the give and take between Brian and J.B.

"I may sign up with Harry for lessons, too," Bill declared. "Maybe I could give you a little help in our match, J.B., because I'm really sick of losing to these guys all the time." This uncommon show of cockiness surprised his three friends.

With a laugh, J.B. slapped Bill on the back. "That's the spirit, partner."

J.B. drove home with a smile on his face. The last couple of weeks had been great. Finally, he had answers for a lot of the questions that had nagged at him for years. Harry Wilkinson had put on a couple of encouraging clinics, and he was willing to let J.B. come for a day to be certain that he was doing the right thing. He was two weeks away from his first lesson with Harry, and washing over him came the first twinge of optimism he had felt toward his golf game in a year and a half.

5
A Day with Harry

THE MORNING WAS A LITTLE ON THE COOL SIDE—sweater weather—normal at some point during the spring in Tennessee. As J.B. arrived at Fox Run, the players with early tee times were just getting there. He headed to the shop where he had agreed to meet Harry.

"Good mornin', Harry. I really appreciate your doing this. I've been looking forward to watching you in action today."

"As long as you hold up your end of the bargain, J.B., it will work out great. I like your desire to learn." Harry glanced at his watch. "It's time to go to work. My first lesson will be here soon. Let's go to the studio."

The two got in Harry's golf cart, which was loaded with his clubs and training aids. The trip down to the studio was a weaving ride on the cart path among large pine trees lining the driving range. Situated at the end of the range, the coach's studio had everything a golfer needed. There was a short game area with a large sand bunker. On the left side of the range starting at 20 yards out, five large barrels were set up at an angle in 20-yard increments. J.B. understood that these were for practicing wedge shots of 100 yards or less. There also was a medium-sized pine tree standing right in the middle of the range about 50 yards out. J.B. wondered what it was for, but he figured he would ask later. Another mystery to him was the purpose of a hilly area in the middle of the practice tee.

They walked into the studio, and J.B. noticed the huge, blown-up swing sequences of past great players like Ben Hogan, Mickey Wright and Sam Snead. The current swings of Steve Elkington and Nick Price were also prominently displayed. Part of Harry's video equipment was on a cart, and he began wheeling it out for the day's lessons. He also had a TV and VCR set up for viewing swings inside the studio. There was a large mirror on the wall facing the entrance and a smaller one on the side wall. There was plenty of room to swing in front of these mirrors. Harry had some of his awards on the wall to the left. He had been named the 1985 National Teacher of the Year by the professional organization to which he belonged, in addition to many local awards. There was also a plaque distinguishing him as one of America's top 50 teachers from a national golf magazine.

Harry's 8:00 lesson had just arrived, and J.B. had a chance to greet her. "Good morning, I'm J.B. Hawkins and I'll be standing back observing today. I hope you don't mind."

"No, not at all. I'm Gina Rumbaugh," she said warmly as she extended her hand. "Harry teaches us to block out distractions by being focused on the task at hand. I won't even notice you're here."

"Well, that's good. I just want to learn some more before my lessons begin next week, and Harry has been gracious enough to let me do this. How long have you been taking lessons?"

"I started a year ago, and I've dropped my handicap from a thirty to an eighteen. My short game handicap has dropped from thirty-two to nineteen."

"Your short game handicap? What's that?"

"Harry gives all of his students a short game skills test and then takes the scores and turns them into handicaps according to a chart that he has. He keeps track of my improvement by giving me the test every so often. I took it last week, and I was better in every category. It feels great to see all the improvement!"

"I've never heard of that. I guess I'll get it next week. You sound excited about the whole thing."

"I'm past excited. I came to my first lesson excited because I had heard of Coach's reputation. I left that lesson ecstatic. Harry has a way of painting a very clear picture of your improvement and pumping you up along the way."

"I've noticed that. Hey, it's time for your lesson. I'll just be hanging around." J.B. shook her hand again and walked toward the spot that Harry had set up.

"I see that you two have met." Harry beamed. "Okay, Gina, let's get started." Harry asked her questions about what she had worked on the most since their last lesson and how everything had been going. He watched her warm up and hit balls, then determined his course of action. J.B. realized that Harry's years of experience made this part second nature. As the lesson continued, J.B. could see what made Harry so good. His explanations were so clear and to the point. When he demonstrated both the correct and incorrect movements, he was so animated and energetic. His enthusiasm was contagious, which made the student want to get better.

J.B. saw this pattern all day long, as students came with a sense of anticipation and left thrilled. At 1:00, Harry held his clinic, which received a fantastic response, as usual.

Harry's students were a cross section of players. On this particular day, he worked with a junior, a beginner, a couple of senior men, a couple of women, and a low single-digit handicapper. When the day wound down, J.B. had a chance to talk to Harry some more.

"Thanks again. This was a thrill to watch. I hope I didn't get in your way," J.B. said.

"I almost didn't notice that you were here," Harry said with a hearty laugh. "Each person you saw today has conquered at least one major swing fault and is rapidly lowering both handicaps, their regular handicap and their short game handicap."

"Oh, yeah. I'm glad I've got a chance to ask you. What is a short game handicap?" J.B. inquired.

Harry chuckled. "This is an idea I borrowed from PGA professionals Conrad Rehling and Jerry Tucker. Conrad was the first person I saw do extensive skill testing, and Jerry was the first person I heard talk about short game handicapping. I give a short game skills test with six categories to my students, then convert each individual category score and the overall score to a handicap, using a chart that I'll give you today before you leave. For a golf student, it makes more sense to have a handicap than an arbitrary number. I then test the player periodically to check for improvements."

J.B. blinked his eyes and nodded, thinking he got the idea but not quite sure.

Harry laughed. "An example would be if Gina gets sixteen points in the short putting skill. That would make her a six-handicap putter. In the bunker let's say she got zero points, which would make her a twenty-handicap bunker player. This gives her an idea of relative strength in each skill and motivates her to improve her score for next time. I've modified the test and handicapping some, but the basic idea came from Conrad and Jerry."

"That's a great idea!" J.B. said enthusiastically.

"I wish I could take credit for it, but it's borrowed, like a lot of them. I'm always looking for the best ideas so that I can continue to improve what we're doing here at Fox Run."

"I bet most people don't like taking the test at first."

"That's right. The players don't like it the first time they take it, but when you can see and measure your improvement, it's a motivator. You'll be taking the test next Saturday."

"Is there anything I should do to prepare?"

"No, I actually want you to come with what you have at the moment, so that we have a good idea of what we need to work on."

"One more thing. I've never heard of a pro who doesn't do one-time lessons. I was surprised when I found out you only do long-term programs."

"Well, I've found that these programs are the only way to accomplish long term success. And if you talk to any of my students, I'm sure they'll agree. Here"—he handed a thick folder to J.B.—"I want you to read the information in this package before our lesson next week."

J.B. opened the folder and pulled out several flyers, reading the titles and glancing at the texts. He noted that there was a USGA rule book enclosed, too, along with a sheet on basic etiquette. As he returned them to the folder, the pleasure was evident on his face. "This is what I want. A clear picture of how the lessons are going to go," he said, excitement filling his voice.

"That's why I put this packet of information together. I'm not a miracle worker, and neither are any of the other people who teach golf. We must change the way people think about learning golf. My six-lesson program is just the start of a long-term relationship with my students. One-time lessons give students the wrong impression," Harry concluded.

"That makes a lot of sense," J.B. agreed.

As they were talking, Harry was putting everything back in its proper place in the studio. They got in the cart and headed back to the clubhouse.

"Harry, thanks again for a super day."

"I'll see you next Saturday, champ," Harry said, planting a seed for the future, "and come an hour early so Lenny can handicap your short game."

"Okay! I look forward to next week."

As soon as J.B. got home, he sat down with the package, titled "New Student Packet." He leafed through the rule book, then pulled out the flyers, beginning to read the first one.

UnCommon Golf

What to Expect From a Master Golf Instructor

1. There is a program for improvement, not just single lessons. Goals will be set, and a realistic time frame given.
2. A short game skills test will be turned into an understandable short game handicap.
3. Your equipment will be checked to make sure you have, at the very least, the proper lie angle, shaft length and shaft flex.
4. The student will be given a set of basic stretching exercises.
5. The instructor will check for physical limitations.
6. There will be equal emphasis on the short game and the full swing.
7. Top instructors will teach the game of golf, not just the swing. This includes the mental side, course management, speed of play, rules and etiquette
8. Concepts will be explained, demonstrated and shown in an understandable manner and in bite-size pieces. Information overload will be avoided.
9. The student will be given drills and/or training aids that will turn these concepts into habits.
10. The instructor will use video analysis as a feedback tool. When used properly, video is a huge help in bridging the gap between fact and feel.
11. The instructor will convey a passion for the game of golf.

J.B. felt a wave of hope mixed with trepidation wash over him. He had gotten himself into a real program here. Very little would be left to chance. He picked up the second flyer.

UnCommon Golf
How To Know
If You have Chosen A Poor Instructor

1. He sells you on quick fixes.
2. He focuses exclusively on the full swing.
3. He comes late or unprepared for the lesson.
4. You are told something like, "You have eight swing faults, and we might be able to work on one of them today."
5. Your equipment is not checked.
6. There is no evaluation of your flexibility.
7. The instructor hits more balls than you do.
8. You are given the entire method in one lesson.
9. You are told their way is the only way or the best way.

**If you are taking lessons
from someone like this,
FIND ANOTHER INSTRUCTOR.
To identify the right person,
use the attributes of a Master Instructor
specified in accompanying handout.**

J.B. groaned. *Oh, brother, why couldn't I have read this before I met Jack Pierce?* He picked up the third flyer.

UnCommon Golf
Short Game Skills Test

PURPOSE: To accurately evaluate your present skill level using a scoring system. This test allows you to have a measurable account of your progress.

BUNKER SHOT—10 Shots
(any lie)

SHOT	POINTS
holed	3
0-5 ft	2
5-10 ft	1
10-15 ft	0
over 15 ft	-1

Bunker Shot Score _____

WEDGE SHOT—10 Shots
(2 from: 20, 40, 60, 80, 100 yds)
where the ball *lands*

SHOT	POINTS
hit target	3
0-10 ft	2
10-20 ft	1
20-30 ft	0
over 30 ft	-1

Wedge Shot Score _____

PITCH SHOT—10 Shots
(15 yds from edge of green, 10-15 yds to the hole)

SHOT	POINTS
holed	3
0-5 ft	2
5-10 ft	1
10-15 ft	0
over 15 ft	-1

Pitch Shot Score _____

LAG PUTTING—10 putts
(2 from: 20, 30, 40, 50, 60 ft)

SHOT	POINTS
holed	3 pts
0-3 ft	2 pts
3-6 ft	1 pt
6-9 ft	0 pts
over 9 ft	-1 pt

Lag Putting Score _____

CHIP SHOT—10 shots from fringe
(5 from 40 ft; 5 from 50 ft)

SHOT	POINTS
holed	3
0-3 ft	2
3-6 ft	1
6-9 ft	0
over 9 ft	-1

Chip Shot Score _____

PUTTING SKILLS—20 putts
left to right 2 putts from 3, 6, 9, 12, 15 ft
right to left 2 putts from 3, 6, 9, 12, 15 ft
2 pts for every putt made

Putting Skills Score _____

TOTAL SCORE _____

Short Game
Handicapping System
A handicap is assigned for each skill score, as well as a handicap for overall score. In the following table, scratch is indicated by ## and points = handicap.

Short Game Handicapping System

Bunker	Wedge	Pitch	Lag Putting	Chipping	Putting	Overall Handicap
20=+5	20=+5	22=+5	24=+5	22=+5	26=+5	107+=+
18=+3	18=+3	20=+3	22=+3	20=+3	24=+3	106=##
16=##	16=##	18=##	20=##	18=##	20=##	95-99=2
15=1	15=1	17=1	18=2	17=2	18=3	90-94=3
14=2	14=3	16=2	17=4	16=4	16=6	85-89=4
13=3	13=4	15=4	16=6	15=6	14=9	80-84=5
12=4	12=5	14=5	15=8	14=8	12=12	75-79=7
11=5	11=7	13=7	14=10	13=10	10=15	70-74=9
10=6	10=9	12=8	13=12	12=12	8=18	65-69=11
9=7	9=10	11=10	12=14	11=14	6=21	60-64=13
8=8	8=12	10=11	11=16	10=16	4=24	55-59=15
7=9	7=14	9=13	10=18	9=18	2=27	50-54=18
6=10	6=16	8=14	9=20	8=20	0=30	45-49=20
5=11	5=18	7=16	8=22	7=22		40-44=23
4=12	4=20	6=18	7=24	6=24		35-39=26
3=14	3=22	5=20	6=26	5=26		30-34=28
2=16	2=24	4=22	5=28	4=28		25-29=30
1=18	1=26	3=24	4=30	3=30		20-24=33
0=20	0=28	2=26	3=32	2=32		15-19=36
-1=22	-1=30	1=28	2=34	1=34		10-14=39
-2=24	-2=32	0=30	1=36			
-3=26	-3=34	-1=32				
-4=30	-4=36	-2=34				
-5=32		-3=36				
-6=34						
-7=36						

As J.B. scanned the handicapping system, he sighed again. *Boy, my bunker score should be interesting*, he thought. He picked up the fourth flyer.

UnCommon Golf
The Proper Use of Video in Golf Instruction

When used correctly, video is a great tool to use in improving a golfer's game. Some people have given video a bad reputation by saying it causes 'paralysis by analysis.' This happens only when an instructor or student uses video incorrectly. By picking out too many faults, the teacher overloads the student and makes them aware of too many things. When an instructor uses it as a feedback tool to bridge the gap between fact and feel, tremendous progress can be made. Here's what to look for when receiving video instruction:

1. The instructor will pick one or two things to focus on during the lesson.
2. He will explain how this affects your golf swing or short game and then suggest the changes.
3. You will then exaggerate the new feeling while being videotaped. This will let you know if you are doing it enough.
4. You stay focused on this new feeling until it becomes a habit.

By using this procedure, you will be able to match up what you **feel** (which can often fool you) with the **facts** that you see on videotape.

J.B. was thoughtful as he put down the flyer and picked up the etiquette sheet.

UnCommon Golf

Basic Etiquette in Golf

Etiquette is an important part of the fabric of golf. Being courteous and showing sportsmanship are two of the benchmarks that make golf great. The following is a list of suggestions for golf etiquette.

1. On the tee, stand where the person hitting the shot cannot see you with his peripheral vision.
2. Play by "honor." The person who had the low score on the previous hole tees off first on the next tee.
3. Pace of play is very important. Play without delay. Try to keep your round under four hours.
4. Do not talk or move while a player is getting ready to hit a shot.
5. On the green, do not walk on another player's line; stand at a place where you do not distract while the other players are putting.
6. Rake the bunkers.
7. Replace your divots.
8. Fix any pitch marks that you make on the green.
9. Do not have dangerous shows of anger such as club throwing or club breaking. Such acts have actually led to the death of golfers.

By following these guidelines, the round of golf will be more enjoyable for everyone.

J.B. sat back, thinking about his day with Coach and contemplating the flyers he had just read. Although he was a grown man, J.B. felt a little in awe of Harry. His mannerisms, voice and general presence on the practice tee exuded enthusiasm and confidence. It didn't take much time around Coach Wilkinson to understand how passionate he was about making his students better players and able to enjoy this game for life. His excitement was contagious, and J.B. was not immune.

6
Where Do We Start?

On Saturday morning, J.B. awoke with a sense of anticipation and hope. Hope about his golf game was something J.B. had not felt in a very long while. So much of his golfing life had been spent feeling hopeless about his slice and his constant mis-hits; hopeless about the tips that seemed to make sense but fell by the wayside in terms of results; hopeless after trying the equipment sold on television that was "guaranteed to hit the ball farther and straighter or your money back"; hopeless after buying the infomercial charlatan's secret video with the promise of learning golf in "one bucket of balls," only to realize that he had been ripped off again.

In fact, J.B. had felt hopeless about his game in general until he met Harry. He was ready for his lesson today, and he knew that he finally had someone who could show him the way. He knew that Harry could point him in the right direction. His lesson was scheduled for 11:00, and he could hardly wait.

Harry had told him to come an hour early, but J.B. decided to get to Fox Run a couple of hours early to get some practice in before doing the short game skills test. As soon as he arrived and got a bucket of balls, he began to work on the ideas he had gotten at the clinics for the past month. To get rid of the slice, he made sure that the clubface was pointed to the left at impact. He also was trying to get his hands ahead at impact to hit it more solidly.

The mixed results J.B. got made him even more ready for the lesson. He headed down to Harry's studio to do the skills test. Harry was finishing up with his 9:00 lesson, and from the player's expression it looked like another success.

"I'll see you in a month, and I want to see that pull path completely gone by then," Harry said with emphasis. The player nodded and continued to practice.

"Mornin' Harry, are you ready for me?"

"Hello, J.B. We have a lot to accomplish today during your first lesson. You need to stretch and then go with Lenny for the short game skills test. We start each week with stretching, because flexibility is critical for you to improve without injury, and it also allows you to make the proper pivot without restriction. Let me show you a basic stretching routine."

Harry had J.B. do a variety of stretches, and J.B. realized that he had some work to do in this area. "Go with Lenny now," Harry said, "and I'll see you at eleven." Harry strode away to start his 10:00 lesson, and J.B. walked over to Lenny.

Under Harry's tutelage, Lenny Griffin had developed into a very successful teacher. When new students came, it was Lenny's job to give them the skills test, which consisted of chipping from two different distances, lag putting, putting from three feet to 15 feet, bunker play, pitching from two spots and controlling wedge distance from 100 yards and in.

When Lenny said, "We'll start with putting," J.B. stepped up with some reservation, knowing his putting was a little suspect. After making only five out of 20, he saw the need for a lot of improvement. His lag putting wasn't too bad, with a score of 16, but the rest of the categories weren't very good, especially the bunker. *If this is the easiest shot in golf*, J.B. thought, *then my game is in big trouble*. His bunker score was minus four.

After the test was over, Lenny showed J.B. how to convert the numbers to handicaps, using the chart in the studio. Overall, he was a 23 handicap in the test, and his worst category was the bunker, in which he was a 30-handicapper.

"It isn't much fun to see how bad I am," J.B. admitted.

"It's not much fun now, but it pays big dividends down the road," Lenny replied. "It gives us a starting point, a measuring stick for your improvement. When you take it again, you're going to love seeing the progress."

J.B. was sure Lenny had made that explanation many times before. "I hope so," J.B. said, trying hard to smile, "because it sure feels lousy right now."

"I also need you to fill out a questionnaire in the studio before your lesson." Lenny handed him a clipboard with a questionnaire and a pencil. "This gives us essential information such as goals, physical limitations and your most common swing thoughts, and it helps us tailor the instruction to your needs. Harry will want to take a look at it at the start of your lesson."

"Hey, you guys think of everything," J.B. said as he headed over to Harry's teaching area, carrying the clipboard and his clubs. He had bought the clubs a few years back after getting a recommendation from a friend, finding them on consignment at a store that sold golf and musical equipment. They were the original Ping Eyes, the smaller head design that, obviously, came out before the Eye 2s. The clubs had black dots on the back of the clubs, which signified standard lie angle, though J. B. wasn't really sure what that meant. He filled out the questionnaire and was ready for his lesson.

"Well, J.B., how did you do?" Harry smiled broadly.

"Not very good, but Lenny says it gives me a good starting point."

"He's right, of course. You'll be better off knowing your weak spots now, and then seeing your handicap improve. You'll also see this show up in your results on the golf course." Harry's authoritative voice gave his statements even more credibility. "Once the skills test is done, the next thing we do here is check your equipment. Have you ever been fitted for the right clubs?"

"No. I just bought these over at Tommy Paul's golf store."

"Okay. The way we do this is, we check the lie angle of your club, which is the angle between the shaft and the bottom edge of the club." Harry held a club up and pointed out the angle. "This is different depending on your height and other features. I'll put electrical tape on the bottom of your clubs and have you hit off of the lie board." Harry pointed to a polyurethane board in front of them while applying tape to J.B.'s five-iron.

"I wondered what that board was used for," J.B. commented as he stepped up to the board. He hit several shots that, invariably, floated to the right. He had to catch himself from falling off balance. He looked at the mark on the tape, and it was toward the toe of the club. "What does this mean?" he inquired.

"It means your lie angles are too flat, which would make your ball fly more to the right. We have to fix this, so we can systematically eliminate the factors that cause the ball to go off-line. Once you know you have properly fitted equipment, we will know that your slice is not caused by your equipment. I'm sorry to say that you got taken on these clubs."

Harry pulled his keys from his pocket and used one of them to scrape the black dot on the club. The paint came off and revealed another color.

"Someone painted the black dots over the gold dots. These are five degrees flat, which is much flatter than you need."

Harry attached a magnetic pointer to the face of J.B.'s club to show the effect that lie angle has on ball flight. "Clubs that are too upright accentuate the ball going to the left. Clubs that are too flat accentuate the ball going to the right." He got J.B.'s lie angle measurement. The fit continued, with Harry determining the proper shaft flex, shaft length and grip size. He then recommended a set make up for J.B.

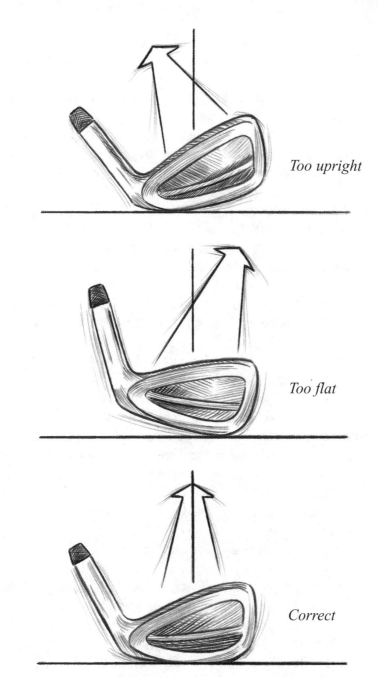

Too upright

Too flat

Correct

"Clubs that are too upright accentuate the ball going to the left. Clubs that are too flat accentuate the ball going to the right."

"Here are your specs, so we can get you into the right equipment," Harry said as he gave J.B. the information on ordering through the club-fitting company he used. "For the time being, I'll get Lenny to bend the clubs after the lesson so you'll have the correct lie angle. Fortunately we don't hit many balls during this first lesson."

"That sounds good." J.B. was ready for any change that would help get rid of his slice.

Harry picked up J.B.'s questionnaire and began to read the answers his new student had written. "J.B., I can tell by the questionnaire that you have very high goals."

"Yes, I'd like to become the best player I can. I'm fed up with being mediocre," J. B. stated matter-of-factly. "I wouldn't mind hitting it farther and straighter, either."

"So, you're not asking for much." Harry chuckled. "Let me explain how the lessons are going to go. I'm a developmental teacher, so I love it when students come with high goals. My job is to give you the best information available, give you drills to form a habit, and then give you feedback on whether you are doing it correctly. Golf has had an aura of quick fixes and tips, which has led to a lot of disappointment, because quick fixes don't lead to long-term improvement. The belief that there is a secret out there that will allow you to improve immediately without practicing is an obvious fallacy. Let me ask you a question. If you were going to take up martial arts, what would you do first?"

"I'd find the best martial arts instructor in my area and start training with him," J.B. said without hesitation.

"You didn't even have to think about it. It's that obvious. It should be that obvious with golf as well," Harry declared.

"You know, my wife made a similar analogy with our daughter's learning to play the piano. Why is finding a teacher not considered as obvious in golf?" J.B. inquired.

"I believe there are a couple of reasons. One, I think a lot of people have read about the self-taught greats of golf. Another reason is that golf has not had a recognized pattern of instruction for the learner. But whatever the reason, seeking out a master instructor should become the first step to golf improvement," Harry said, accentuating his words with a fist pounded into his hand.

"That makes a lot of sense," J.B. agreed.

"We're going to learn golf the same way a person learns piano or martial arts: one skill at a time, in a progression from simple to complex. What is the first thing your daughter would learn in piano lessons?"

"First how to sit, then the keys and the scales, then how to read music," J.B. quickly reeled off.

"In golf, it's our basics. During our one-hour lessons, we will work on your full swing and short game equally. There are actually more short game shots during your round than full swing shots. You've heard that defense wins championships in other sports, haven't you?"

"Of course."

"Short game is the defense that wins championships in golf. We will have two tracks during each lesson. Short game, which starts with putting, and full swing, which starts with grip, aim and setup. I'll make the learning process fun, but—as in any worthy endeavor—there's some work involved. Do you have any other questions before we continue?"

"No, I don't. What's next?"

Harry continued to look at the questionnaire. "I see that you had lessons. Who was your instructor?"

"Jack Pierce, but that's a sore subject. I didn't want anything to do with teachers after that experience." J.B.'s voice had a hint of anger.

"It's important that I find out the key swing thoughts that have led to your swinging the way you do now. Could you show me what Jack showed you?"

J.B. showed Harry the wide stance with no knee flex. He showed him the large weight shift to the right and the club dropping parallel to the ground as it started forward. He then went to the awkward, twisted-hip finish.

"He seems to have shown you a good grip and a good idea for aim." Harry looked at J.B.'s straight-legged address, "We'll work on that posture today. The rest of the swing will come in future lessons. What other ideas have you worked on a lot?"

"Keeping my head down was a big one before I went to your clinic. And staying slow and relaxed," J.B. answered.

"You've probably been told to take the club 'straight back and straight through'," Harry deduced.

"Now that you say it, I have. How did you know that?" J.B. was impressed. ·

"Thoughts become actions. From your actions, I know what thoughts led to them. Any misconceptions are going to show up as bad habits and hinder your success. I'm going to be giving you correct concepts that lead to good habits."

"That sounds great."

"That's why I asked you about your lessons with Jack, but that's as far as we need to delve into that situation," Harry said.

"Sounds good," J.B. agreed.

"Okay. Now that we've given you the skills test and checked your equipment, I need to have you do a couple of things to check for physical limitations." At this point Harry checked for flexibility in J.B.'s upper chest, hips and right arm and left arm, shoulder and wrist. "Everything looks pretty good. You lack some flexibility in your upper chest turn, so I'll give you some exercises to increase that. Flexibility can have a major effect on your pivot, so it's very important. Now, let's work on your foundation—grip, aim and set up. Let me see you set up with a seven-iron to get an idea of where you are right now."

J.B. grabbed his seven-iron and lined up toward the yellow flag that was in the middle of the range about 150 yards away.

"How does it look, Harry?" inquired J.B.

"It's not bad, J.B., but we can make it better. In teaching, I am dealing with constants and variables. The more variables your swing has, the more reasons why you miss your shots. As the fundamentals we work on become ingrained, the reasons for missed shots become manageable. If you have correct grip, aim and set-up, it does not insure a straight shot. It insures that your grip, aim and set-up are not the reason for the missed shot. You can then figure out what to focus on to get rid of your slice. For example, imagine the person who hits a slice and has a weak grip, alignment right, slouched posture, out-to-in path and a reverse pivot. After they slice it, where do they start to find the solution? There is no obvious starting point because there were too many variables. However, if you take care of the grip, aim and set-up, that eliminates three possibilities for the slice, and you know that it was something in your swing."

These were the best, most understandable explanations J.B. had ever heard. He had to make the fundamentals second nature. "What do I need to do on my grip, aim and set-up?" he asked.

"Let's talk about the grip, first of all. I believe the grip has three functions: to hinge the club, square the face, and give support at the top of the swing. First, I have a drill for you to do to accomplish the hinging of the club," said Harry. He demonstrated a drill in which the club was held in the left hand with the heel pad on top of the club and the forefinger only. He then moved the club up and down. "Let's see you do the same thing."

"Jack gave me this same drill," J.B. said as he performed the drill.

"Good. Then you're already on your way to a good grip," Harry said. "There you go. Now, move it up and down."

J.B. hinged the club properly.

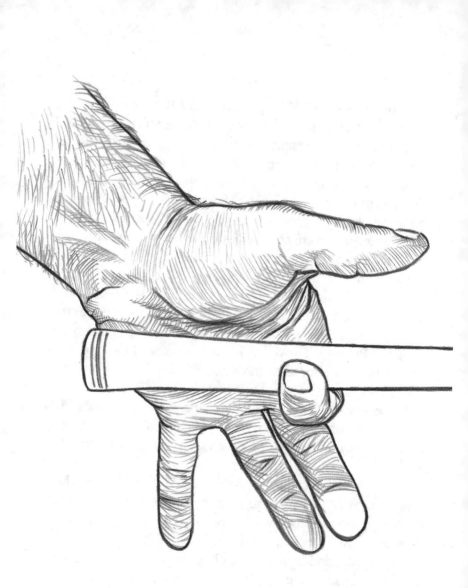

"First, I have a drill for you to do to accomplish the hinging of the club . . ."

Harry continued, "When you wrap your three fingers and put the club in front of you, I want you to be able to see two or three knuckles on your left hand."

J.B. could see three knuckles. "Is that too strong?" J.B. asked.

"No," Harry replied. "Four-knuckle grips are what we call strong, and one-knuckle or no-knuckle grips are what we call weak. Your grip is right where I want it. Now, your right hand should be on the side of the club." Harry demonstrated this and also put J.B.'s hand in the correct position.

"The way we put our hands on the club allows us to do the second function we talked about, which is to square the face."

"Is this right?" J.B. pushed his hands out for Harry to check.

"Yes, that's very good. Now take the club to the top."

J.B. did as Harry asked.

"The club should be supported by your left thumb and the pad of your right forefinger." Harry again demonstrated and adjusted J.B. accordingly. "You now have a correct, functional grip," said Harry.

"It doesn't feel that much different, but it certainly makes more sense to me now," J.B. commented, removing his hands and then taking his grip several times to get a feel for it.

"Now, on to aim," Harry said. "Most people line the shoulders up to the target, which in turn lines them up to the right of the target." Harry demonstrated while holding a club across his shoulders. "Answer an obvious question for me. What hits the ball?"

"The club," said J.B.

"That's close. The clubface, to be exact. So, what needs to be lined up to the target?"

"The clubface."

"That's right. Clubface first, body second. That's a principle I want you to ingrain into your pre-shot routine—the face lined up directly at the target. Here's another key concept: the body is parallel, left of the target."

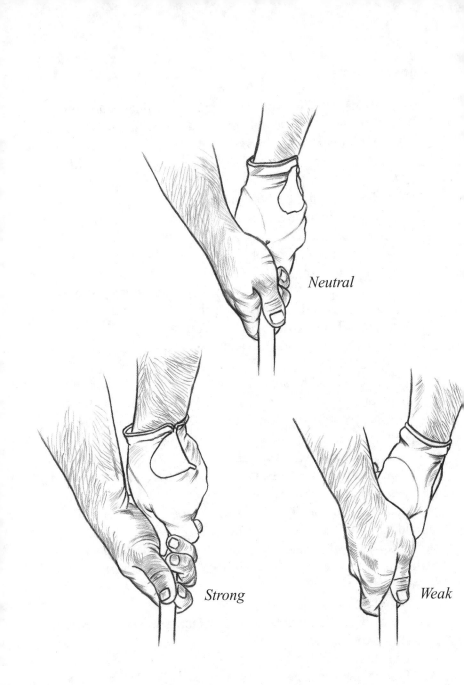

Neutral

Strong

Weak

"Four-knuckle grips are what we call strong, and one-knuckle or no-knuckle grips are what we call weak."

At this point Harry put two shafts on the ground. One was pointed at the target and the other was parallel to the target shaft. J.B. recognized this same drill from Jack's lesson. Harry set up with the face at the target and his feet, knees, hips and shoulders parallel, but not at the flag. He put a shaft across his shoulders to show where they pointed. J.B. could see the difference, now, between pointing your shoulders at the target and correctly pointing them parallel to the target.

"This takes some work and feedback to become good at, because we stand sideways in golf and are dealing with a visual distortion. That's why I want you to set up a practice station of shafts for alignment so that you will become good at this."

"I think my alignment is pretty good," J.B. said, while standing in his station of shafts.

"It is. You developed good alignment and grip in your lessons with Jack. Let's move to the third part of your foundation, the set-up. We're going to focus mainly on posture today. Let me give you three reasons why you should develop good posture. One, bad posture restricts your arm movement. Two, bad posture restricts your body turn. And three, bad posture leads to injuries."

Harry demonstrated a slouched, curved spine, showing how it restricted arm movement and body turn. He had J.B. perform the same movements.

"Now, let me explain how bad posture causes injuries," Coach said. "Your spine is shaped like this . . ." Harry used J.B.'s back to show that when standing straight the back has a very small s-shaped curve. "When you have good posture, the spine is healthy, and there should be a small gap between the vertebrae." He used his thumb and forefinger to show a small gap.

"Between vertebrae there is tissue called a disc, which acts as a cushion. When our posture gets slouched forward, the vertebrae touch, and the discs get squeezed and pinched. Now,

"One of the main principles here is that we bend from the hips, not the waist."

you take a backswing and the vertebrae are grinding on each other and pinching the discs. This happens shot after shot after shot for years. The discs get inflamed and back pain kicks in. Eventually, you can't even play because of the pain. Now, do you see why it's important to have good posture?" Harry chuckled as he asked the question.

"Wow, that's a bleak picture. In that case, I guess I should probably have good posture," J.B. said, mockingly returning Harry's good humor.

"Okay, let me show you how. One of the main principles here is that we bend from the hips, not the waist. If you literally bend from the waist your spine will be just as I described it, curved the wrong way and headed for injury. The drill that we will use is the 'club down your back' drill."

Harry put a club behind his back to demonstrate the drill. The club rested at his belt loop, between his shoulder blades and the back of his head. When he bent from the hips his back stayed straight. He had J.B. do the same thing.

"How does that feel, J.B.?" asked Harry.

"Awkward, but I know my posture hasn't been very good. I also feel as though my weight is on my toes," commented J.B.

"It is. Now, what I want you to do is get just enough knee flex to be balanced. If I give you a light push on the shoulders forward and then back, you should not be pushed over easily." Harry gave J.B. a push, and J.B. did not move forward, although he was rocked a little backward.

"That's a sign that your weight was on your heels, which means you overcompensated with too much knee flex. Get a little less knee flex this time."

Harry checked J.B. again after the adjustment, and his balance was rock solid.

"Now, you're in an athletic, balanced position to start your swing," Harry said. "There are only a couple of other things. First, when you take your grip, your right hand is lower than your left on the club and, correspondingly, your right shoulder should be lower than your left. I call this slight tilt of the upper body 'secondary angle,' and we try to maintain it throughout the swing. Let me see you do it."

J.B. clumsily tried to get the slight tilt.

Harry adjusted him. "That's great! Right there," Harry exclaimed with the excitement he got from watching his students put his concepts into practice. "Then we need to put your ball in a good position. I'm not going to go into all the theory on ball position. Too far forward or back causes problems, so trust me to put your ball in the right spot so that it gets in the way of your soon-to-be good swing. Put it right here." Harry pointed to a spot just in front of J.B.'s sternum.

"I think I can handle that. . . . So, let me see if I'm doing this right," J.B. said. "I take the grip like this"—J.B. showed Harry the hinge drill, then put both hands on the club—"aim the clubface first, then put my body parallel." J.B. put his club behind the ball and then aligned his body. "Put the ball right here, and make sure I bend from the hips and am balanced." J.B. completed his set-up.

"That's super. Now, just do it enough times that it becomes second nature. By our next lesson this will be a habit."

"Should the secondary angle normally make me feel as though I'm leaning this far to the right?" J.B. wondered aloud.

"When your tendency has been to set up with your shoulders level, it will. Let me show you how it looks." Harry turned on his video camera, which was positioned to view J.B. from the front. "Come here and look at it," Harry said as he flipped out the little 3.5-inch screen to show J.B.

"I can't believe it. I'm only tilted a little. It feels like this much." J.B. bent to the right as though he were doing a side bend.

"First, when you take your grip, your right hand is lower than your left on the club and, correspondingly, your right shoulder should be lower than your left. I call this slight tilt of the upper body 'secondary angle,' and we try to maintain it throughout the swing."

"Exactly. You just need to keep doing it until you don't have to think about it," Harry declared. "Now, it's time for the second half of the lesson. Putting."

J.B. looked at his watch. He couldn't believe they had already been working for thirty minutes. "Grab your putter and come to the green," Harry said.

When J.B. got to the green, he noticed that there were three-foot radius circles painted around the holes. There were also blue chalk lines on three of the holes. There were strings attached to pencils that made straight lines to the hole, and there were two four-foot long two-by-fours sitting on their edges. J.B. had not seen them during his skills test, so he knew Lenny must have brought them out while Harry was teaching him the pre-swing.

"Okay, I looked at your skills test score of 10 points, which makes you a 15-handicap putter. Let me watch you putt some six-footers."

J.B.'s putts went in the general vicinity of the hole, but only a couple were going in. His putter seemed to waiver, and he was unsure of his alignment.

"Just as I suspected. Your alignment is inconsistent, and so is your stroke. Have you ever used alignment aids, such as these chalk lines or two-by-fours?"

"No."

"I didn't think so, but these tools are not common knowledge. Let's talk about the physics of making a putt. The face must be pointed to your intended target to get the ball to go there. It is easier to deliver the face with a simple, straight-back and straight-through path. This is the *only* time you will hear me mention that phrase, because nothing in golf is straight back and straight through except for short putts. I'll explain that more, later. You also need to hit the sweet spot of the putter to develop feel. Let me show you how to find the sweet spot."

Harry held his putter up and used his forefinger to tap the putter, starting at the heel. As he tapped, the putter twisted. As he moved toward the center of the putter face and tapped, the twist was less and less until he found a spot toward the center where it did not twist. As he continued to tap toward the toe, the putter resumed its twist.

"Where the putter did not twist is the sweet spot," Coach explained. "As you can imagine, this would be the most consistent spot on your putter to hit your putts. We use specific training aids and drills to develop the ability to have your face pointed toward your intended target at impact. One of the reasons putting is not as easy as it looks is because we don't stand behind the ball with both eyes looking toward the target. We have to stand sideways and glance over at the hole, which gives us a distorted image."

"Can you stand behind and putt like you're using a croquet mallet?" J.B. inquired.

"Sam Snead used to do that successfully, but it was outlawed by a rule of golf that will not allow you to straddle the line of a putt while making the stroke. So, we have to learn to deal with the distorted image that standing sideways gives us. That's why we will use the drills and training aids that you see here."

Harry pointed to the different stations set up on the putting green. "First we are going to use the two-by-fours to train your path and face." Harry showed J.B. how to let the heel of the club go back and forth against the board to develop a simple stroke. The two-by-fours were lined up to the hole, and J.B. was amazed at how many went in.

"I should just take one of these on the golf course with me," J.B. exclaimed.

"You practice with these two-by-fours enough, and you'll take these results out to the golf course."

"First we are going to use the two-by-fours to train your path and face."

Harry showed J.B. a basic grip and stance to make him consistent, and then they moved to the chalk line. "This chalk line helps train your eyes to see a straight line while standing sideways, and it helps you learn to line up your putter face to the target."

J.B. hit some putts using the chalk line to help line up. He again noticed that he made more putts. He felt great about the immediate results.

"This proves that if you can learn to line up to the target and return the face square to the target at impact, you can make putts," Harry said. "For most people, aligning to the target is not natural, so it must be learned. That's why we use the drills and training aids. The other factor is speed control, which we will work on in a later lesson."

J.B. continued to practice while Harry gave him feedback.

"This is great, Coach. I've never made this many six-footers," exclaimed J.B. He saw that his earlier attempts to steer, guide, help, shove and force the ball into the hole were totally wasted and unnecessary. Once again, Harry had made a key golf skill seem simple.

Harry beamed. "You train this in, and you'll make a lot more putts. The hour has nearly passed, and I want to finish up with a little pep talk. I'm in the business of concept formation and habit creation. The concepts we talked about today set the groundwork for tomorrow. The rough part is not the lesson, but the practice that has to take place between lessons. It is not about tips and gimmicks. You must now take the information I've given you and turn it into habits through drills," Harry said.

J.B. realized that Harry had given this speech to many students, but he received it in the spirit in which it was given, as a personal message. "I'll work at it, Coach. I've always been willing to work. I just didn't have an idea of what the right things to work on might be. Now, I do. I have one more question. At your clinic a couple of weeks ago, you insisted that

'You're not lifting your head.' That was an eye opener for me. Will we talk about that next time?" asked J.B.

"Yes, we will," Harry replied. "Understanding that concept changes everything. From chipping all the way to the driver, it is the basic understanding of how you use the loft of the club to get the ball into the air. . . . By the way, J.B., did you look through the packet of information that I gave you two weeks ago?"

"I sure did. It was very informative. I had to laugh at some of the traits listed for poor instructors. I could relate to those."

"Did you look at the rule book?"

"I glanced at it."

"J.B., that rule book is the basis for playing golf. The game of golf is a game of integrity. Unlike most sports, we call penalties on ourselves. You have to know the rules to play golf to its fullest. I want you to read it some and keep a copy in your golf bag."

"All right."

"I want to see you again in two weeks. Remember to leave your clubs with Lenny to be bent."

"Great! I'll see you in two weeks, and I'll stop by after work on Monday to pick up my clubs," said J.B. They shook hands and Harry went to have lunch.

J.B.'s passion for golf had been reawakened, and he knew that retaining the clear pictures that were now in his head was critical. Harry had painted a work of art in J.B.'s mind. The brush strokes were clear and distinct, creating a painting that took the place of what had been lifeless, incorrect ideas. The fundamentals of grip, aim and posture were now alive and real to J.B.

The value of a teacher, J.B. thought. Certain teachers had made an impact on J.B. in earlier years. Two high school teachers stood out in particular, one in English and the other in math. It was amazing the way a great teacher could take a lifeless or confusing subject and make it alive and clear. *What a gift. It's ridiculous that golfers don't immediately find one of these teachers. This person can open up a new world, one of clarity, hope and enjoyment.*

The clinics, the day with Harry, and now his first lesson had created just this kind of a firestorm of emotion and energy in J.B. He knew he could learn this game. He wished he had run into Harry when he started playing golf.

7
Loft is the Answer

IN FRONT OF THE HALL MIRROR, J.B. PRACTICED what Harry had taught him. He did not notice when his son came into the hall.

"Daddy, what are you doing?" Nick asked.

"I'm working on my posture, son."

"What's posture?"

"It's how you stand when you're getting ready to hit a golf shot," J.B. responded.

"You've been doing that a lot lately. How come?"

"I'm trying to become a better golfer."

"Can I become a golfer?" Nick asked.

"Sure, come to the garage, and we'll have a little putting contest." They moved to the garage where J.B. had set up a nine-foot putting mat that he had bought the past week. The mat was green Astro-turf with two holes at the end.

"Can I go first?" Nick asked.

"Sure, you can. Let me see you hold the putter." Nick grabbed the putter in an awkward, two-fisted manner. He looked more like he was going to sweep the floor than make a putt. He lined up, stroked the ball, and it went in.

"Good putt, son!"

Nick looked up at his Dad with bright eyes as he received a high-five. "This is fun! Now, let me see you do it, Dad!"

This put some pressure on J.B.'s new stroke. He took his new putting grip and hit the putt. His revamped stroke hit the ball right into the middle of the hole.

"Way to go, Daddy!" Nick cheered as he returned the high-five. "Will you take me to play some time?"

"We'll do that soon," J.B. said with pride. He wanted Nick

to play golf, if it was his son's choice. Now that J.B. had hope for his own game, he could be enthusiastic about sharing golf with Nick.

"Time for dinner," Rachel said as she peeked into the garage.

"We'll be right there, Mom. I'm tied with Daddy," Nick said as he was lining up for another putt.

"Make it quick, so the food doesn't get cold," Rachel replied.

"Let's call it a tie and go to dinner," J.B. proposed.

"Okay. We'll play some more after dinner though, right?" Nick countered.

"You're on," J.B. said as he grabbed Nick and carried him over his shoulder to the kitchen table.

On the Saturday morning of his second lesson, J.B. arrived at Fox Run an hour early to putt and get in a little last-second practice on his grip, aim and set-up. After about half-an-hour of practice, he went over to the attendant to get a cart to ride down to Harry's lesson area. On his way down he saw people hitting on the range. He was able to see some of their mistakes now, and he wondered why they didn't go to Harry or Lenny to take a lesson. *What a shame to waste all that time and effort doing the wrong things and making them into bad habits*, J.B. thought. He continued down the cart path through the trees and arrived about 15 minutes before his 11:00 appointment.

Lenny was busy giving a lesson on the left side of the range where the lone pine tree was located about 50 yards out. Lenny was having his student curve the ball around the tree, mainly from right-to-left. *That's what the tree is for*, J.B. realized. *What a good idea*. The student could learn to curve the ball or hit it high over the tree or low below it's branches. Harry was finishing his 10:00 lesson with some work in the bunker.

J.B. stood in front of the huge mirror in Harry's studio and worked on his posture. J.B. thought it looked good in the

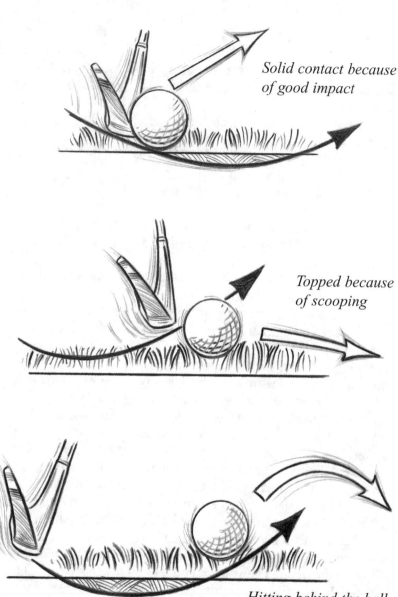

Solid contact because of good impact

Topped because of scooping

Hitting behind the ball because of scooping

"The problem is that the player does not understand how to use a lofted club."

mirror, and it was starting to feel normal. He began to do his stretches. Touching his toes still hurt, just as it did at high school basketball practice. He stopped to look at the photographs of swing sequences in Harry's studio. There was a certain magic to imagining his swing being like theirs. J.B.'s favorite was Steve Elkington. His swing looked athletic and fluid.

"Are you ready to get to work today?" Harry asked, bringing J.B. out of his self-imposed trance.

"I've been ready for this for about thirteen years. I just didn't know it until this past month. I did the stretches," J.B. added as they walked to the tee.

"Good. Let's see how far you've come. Now set up and hit a golf ball."

J.B. went through his new routine. He was a bit rigid, but all the elements looked better. His grip looked like it had been molded onto the club; his alignment routine was clubface first and body second; and his posture was athletic and balanced.

"That's what I wanted to see, J.B. You've obviously practiced, and the reward is the foundation of a good swing. I'll bet your putting is better, too.

"Much better. I'm ready to take that test again," J.B. said.

"We'll do it again in due time. As I told you last time, each hour will consist of half short-game and half full-swing. Today we're going to start with chipping, because it is the shortest swing with a lofted club. You had asked me about the 'You're Not Lifting Your Head' clinic at the end of the last lesson, and this is where it starts. What really happens is not that the head lifts or picks up. The problem is that the player does not understand how to use a lofted club. What makes the ball get in the air?"

"I've heard people say to hit down on it to get the ball up," answered J.B.

"There is a little bit of truth in that statement, but that doesn't explain it clearly enough. The handle of the club should be in front of the club head at impact." Harry demonstrated this position. "This allows the ball to hit the sweet spot, and the loft gets the ball up into the air. Most golfers make an ill-fated attempt to *help* the ball up into the air. The wrist bends, the weight stays on the back foot, and the club catches the ball on the way up. Let me reiterate what I said in the clinic. In 35 years of teaching, I have *never* seen anyone lift his head before impact and top a golf ball. Now, I'm sure there may be an exception out there, but the main point is that it's not the epidemic that you would think by listening to golfers tell each other to keep their heads down," said Harry.

"Your clinic blew my friends away, because they had all told me I was lifting my head. And let me tell you, Harry, we were a little skeptical. But when you explained scooping, it made sense. Now, the key is to get rid of the scooping that I've had for all these years."

"That's right, and that's what brings us to chipping. This is the best place to learn to have ball-compressing impact. Your job as a golfer is to hit the ball solidly and let the loft of the club get it into the air." At this point, they had made their way over to the short game area where Harry had some balls laid out for chipping. "Let me see you chip a couple with your nine-iron."

J.B. grabbed his nine-iron and began to chip. He was attempting to keep the handle ahead and hit the ball with a slight descent, but his wrist would break down at the last second. He hit about 10 balls. Some were thin, a couple he hit behind, and a few felt solid, but they certainly weren't consistent. Harry watched intently before speaking.

"J.B., don't feel discouraged. You and about ninety percent of all golfers do this same thing. With some drills and a couple of training aids, this can be cured. First, let me have you think of hitting the ball under this shaft instead of over it." Harry held up a shaft at about knee height. "Keep your hands more ahead and deloft the club to hit under something."

J.B. made a swing with his hands ahead of the clubhead at impact. He hit the ball solidly, but it went over the shaft. J.B. was surprised.

"How about that? You kept your hands ahead, hit the ball solidly and it actually went over the shaft instead of under. You finally used the loft of the club correctly."

"That felt great! I really hit that ball solid. I haven't felt that very many times since I've been playing golf. I guess that's why I like fluffy lies, so I can get under it," said J.B., as he demonstrated his old scoop move.

Harry chuckled. "You and twenty million other golfers! This should be a required lesson before students go out to play for the first time."

"Hey, there's an idea. It would be like having a driver's license for the golf course."

Harry answered, "Yes, we would also have everyone make their first swings with a good pre-swing and understand the importance of the short game. Each golfer would know the basic rules and etiquette of the game. But licensing golfers is a topic for another time. Let's get back to the lesson."

"Okay," J.B. agreed as he started to practice.

"Keep doing the drill. Feel like you are going to hit it under the shaft with your hands ahead." Harry held out the shaft once again.

J.B. hit shots, with most of them being solid. He felt pretty stiff and awkward, and Harry explained to him that it was normal to feel and look that way. J.B. was encouraged by how solidly he was now hitting the ball. He occasionally scooped, but now he could feel it and knew that he wasn't lifting his head.

"Harry, where do you think the advice 'keep your head down' and 'don't lift your head' came from?" asked J.B.

Harry thought a moment. "It was an attempt to explain something that repeatedly happened. In defense of people who have thought this, without seeing it in slow motion on videotape, it could appear that the person is raising his head. Interestingly enough, if there is something that most golfers do, they keep their head down too long after impact, which restricts their body movement."

Harry paused, then continued. "From the time I started playing golf at ten until I was a pro at twenty-one, I thought golfers lifted their heads. Scooping was explained to me by a great pro named Stan Parsons when I began my career. I've spent the thirty-five years since then dispelling that and many other misconceptions about golf. I cannot stand to watch the fiasco of a novice giving advice to another golfer . . . advice that is wrong, I might add."

Harry's show of frustration was unusual. "Each person who has the desire to improve at golf should, *at the very least*, be given the right ideas to use as he practices. This has been a lifelong goal of mine, and I will continue with it until I retire. Every golfer who wants to get better should be given a chance to reach his or her potential."

"Well, Harry," J.B. said, "I know I came to the right place. My chipping is already much better." J.B. continued to chip with some very nice results.

"It's time to move to the second half of today's lesson, which is a continuation of our work on the full swing." They moved about 30 yards from the short game area to the range. "Let me see you set up for a shot," Harry said.

J.B. grabbed a seven-iron and addressed the ball. It still felt somewhat foreign to him, but not as bad as it had two weeks earlier.

Harry made a couple of small adjustments and then declared, "Well done. You are now ready for our next step: clubface awareness." Harry grabbed a seven-iron and continued. "Most golfers have no awareness of where the clubface is during their swing, much less at impact. I'm going to run you through where the club should be at certain key checkpoints. From the address position, take the club back to parallel with the toe of the club up," Harry said, demonstrating.

Toe-up
Square club face

Closed   *Open*

"From the address position, take the club back to parallel
with the toe of the club up . . ."

J.B. followed suit.

"Good job!" Harry exclaimed.

"When I do this it feels as though I'm taking it inside," J.B. declared.

"We're going to talk about path and swing plane at the next lesson, J.B. It's normal for the correct backswing to feel awkward. Now, the club begins to hinge and the leading edge of the club should be in line with your forearm." Harry continued to demonstrate while J.B. attempted to copy his movements.

"You know, Coach, I take the club back, straight back and then go straight through. No wonder I can't square the face. I've never thought about where the clubface is."

"That's right. Let's continue to the top, and the leading edge will be in line with your left forearm. This would be closed"—Harry bowed J.B.'s wrist so it pointed more to the sky—"and this is open." Harry cupped J.B.'s wrist and the club pointed downward.

J.B. didn't quite have it, so Harry adjusted him. Harry was moving him through the positions to make sure J.B. understood.

"Now the club starts down, and this is where you see the fruits of your labor," continued Harry. "The leading edge will not be laid back in an open position or leaning forward in a closed position. It will be what's called a neutral, or square, position." Harry showed the three different possibilities. "Now, we continue down toward the moment of truth, impact. This is going to be exactly as I showed you earlier in chipping. The handle is leading to hit the ball solidly, and the face is pointed toward the target. The ball jumps off the loft of the face toward the target as you follow through to the toe-up position in the follow through."

Harry showed J.B. the toe-up position in the follow through. "And then . . . on to your finish," Harry said as he finished. "Is the concept of clubface position clear to you now?"

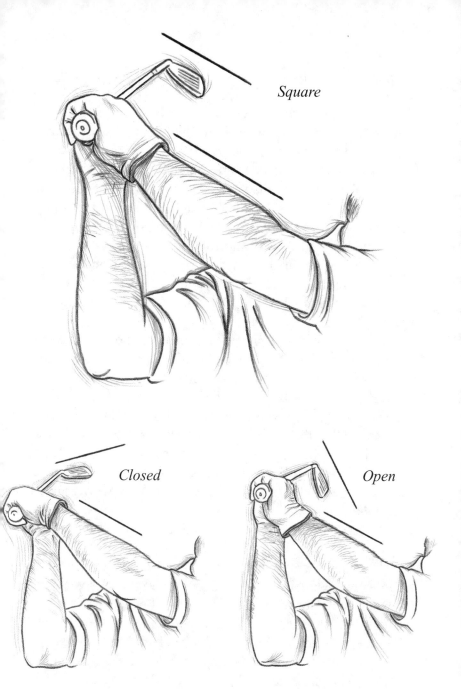

Square

Closed

Open

"This would be closed"—Harry bowed J.B.'s wrist so it pointed more to the sky—"and this is open." Harry cupped J.B.'s wrist and the club pointed downward.

"Now, it is. It was never been clear before how to hit it to the target. I had always wondered why I sliced. Now, I can see why. My face was open at impact."

"Yes. When you make that exaggerated attempt to take the club straight through, the face points to the right of your path, creating side spin that hits the ball to the right. Let me tell you something else. I could completely get rid of all slicing with a combination of this information and what we're going to work on in our next lesson. There would be no more slicing if people took lessons from qualified instructors who showed them about clubface and path. This always gets me on my soapbox, J.B., so bear with me."

Harry grabbed a tennis racket from his bag of training aids. "There are no chronic slicers in tennis. If I were to tell you to hit a cross court forehand, you would release the racquet face to the left, which would send the ball to the left. If I said to hit it down the line, you would 'square' the racket face when you hit the ball, and that would propel the ball down the line." Harry was his usual animated self as he demonstrated with the vigor of a 20-year-old. "I have no students who still slice. I get rid of slicing immediately. At this lesson tee, there is no *slicing* and no *scooping*."

"Why aren't these concepts common knowledge?" J.B. asked.

"Because there is no common knowledge! There are some commonly held misconceptions, but . . . well, that's why I call my company UnCommon Golf. Plenty of people jump in with advice, but those self-styled advisors disagree with each other! So even in that respect, there's no common knowledge." Harry's eyebrows shot up as he concluded, and J.B. laughed.

"Enough philosophy," Harry said, also laughing. "The things I have showed you and will continue to show you are correct concepts and principles. I think many times we see methods and tips that confuse the average golfer because one person says one thing that contradicts what another teacher is saying. These tips are quick fixes that don't change bad habits or create correct ones. Golfers who are serious about getting better and are tired of scooping and slicing *must* find a good teacher and learn the game correctly."

J.B. soaked it all in, then continued hitting balls. He knew he looked a little stiff as he worked on his slice, making sure the face was going in the same direction as his path.

"J.B., how would you hit shots that go way left?"

"I would point the face to the left at impact to do that."

"That's what I wanted to hear. Now I know you understand today's lesson."

J.B. hit shots with the face pointed left. Not only did he get rid of his customary slice, the balls went farther.

"Why did I pick up distance?" J.B. turned to Harry and asked with surprise.

"Because a good impact position delofts the club, and when the face is pointed left instead of right, that also delofts the club. Clubhead speed, centered hits and loft work together to determine distance. That feels better, doesn't it?"

"Feels better? That's the understatement of the day. I'm sure you know how frustrating hitting a slice is, just by seeing the look in your students' faces. This is great!" J.B. continued to hit shots that were solid, longer and left of his intended target. He had a big smile on his face after hitting shots as he never had before.

"How long before I get these shots to go to the target?" asked J.B.

"At our next lesson we're going to talk about path and swing plane. When the path and face are pointed toward the target at impact, the ball will go to the target. You have the face squaring up to the path. We just need the path to be correct so you can hit your shots to the target. I've given you enough to work on for the next couple of weeks. The information has to come in bite-size pieces. So many times people want it all at once, but learning golf or any motor skill doesn't work that way. Do you feel as though you understand what we talked about today?"

"Absolutely! I'm excited about finally getting better at this game. I can tell you that my kids are going to learn the right way, and all my friends who want to get better will be coming to see you, too," said J.B.

"Thanks for the great compliment. I would consider it an honor to teach your children. I cannot stand to watch children learning to hate the game of golf because their well-meaning father took them out and gave them the same ideas that led to his being an eighteen-handicapper. Parents should introduce their kids to the game and if they show an interest, teach them etiquette, then find them a good instructor."

J.B. nodded in agreement.

"I'll schedule you for two weeks from now, and we'll keep building this solid swing. Keep working hard. It's worth it," Harry said as he shook J.B.'s hand and headed to his daily lunch hour.

J.B. continued to practice his newly found drills and techniques. He was committed to exaggerating the handle leading through impact. He could feel his old urge to help the ball into the air, but he used extra effort to hit the ball solidly and let the loft get it up. He chipped a lot of balls and most of them were solid. Harry had not spoken much about distance control, but J.B. was sure they would talk about that later. He could not believe he could make the ball go left. He had done it wrong for so many years, and the correct idea was so obvious that he wondered why it hadn't dawned on him before now. He was hitting the ball so solidly that he did not even feel it come off the face. Things were looking up.

8
The Plane Truth

Two WEEKS COULD NOT PASS FAST ENOUGH FOR J.B. He had always been the type of person who became engrossed in a project or activity, nearly to the point of obsession. The back yard had only taken a small beating from his chip shots, and for his wife's sake he was saving his large divots for the driving range. He played with Brian and the boys on the Saturday following his lesson. Brian and Robby needled J.B. a little harder than usual, maybe because he was breaking out of the ranks of the hacker. He had broken the unspoken rule of the hacker's club, which is that you must never take a lesson. Club members of this unofficial group didn't always take kindly to a defector.

"Nice of you to make it, J.B. We thought you'd be preparing for the Open for the next couple of weeks, with all that money you're spending on lessons," said Brian.

"Keep talking. Your day is coming. It's a little too new for me to get you yet! Mark this day, June fifth, on your calendar for next year. I'll be playing against you and Robby's best ball and giving you strokes," said J.B., serving notice.

"Won't you be playing in that televised Skins match with Woods, Duval and Mickelson that weekend?" Robby asked sarcastically.

"Nah. I'd much rather play with my old pals, the ones who'll be repaying all those dollars I've lost to them in the past," J.B.

said with a grin. For the most part, he ignored their comments as he played. When he did respond, it was with good humor.

J.B.'s set up was looking good, though a little stiff. He was hitting the ball solidly but to the left the whole round because of his new clubface position at impact. He made a swing on his approach to the tenth green at Fox Run, which was surrounded by a water hazard. The pulled shot made a big splash that disturbed a family of ducks. He pulled the ball to the left all day.

There was one very positive thing that happened during the round for J.B. It was the way he played the fifteenth hole. He actually saw a glimpse of some improvement. His clubface squared up, which sent the tee shot 20 yards farther than usual . . . and straight! His approach shot ended up five feet from the hole, and he made the putt for birdie. These were the things Harry had showed him, and they were starting to work. *That's the way I'm going to start playing if I stick with it,* J.B. thought. He finished with a 92, but it was a different 92. He had more penalty shots than normal, and they had all gone left. That was a minor victory in itself.

After the round, they all went to the clubhouse to get their beverage of choice and pay up on bets.

"Well, better luck next time," Brian said as he collected his money.

"Enjoy this while you can. Your day is coming," J.B. reminded Brian.

"Stop it. You're scaring me," Brian said as Robby joined in to laugh at that one.

*   *   *

As J.B. rode toward his third lesson appointment, he saw Harry finishing his 10:00 lesson. He was passionately demonstrating a final point, and even from halfway down the cart path, one could get an idea of what he was trying to convey.

J.B. went through what had become a routine. He went into the studio and checked his progress in the large mirror. The posture was still looking good. He checked his face position checkpoints from the last lesson, then faced the mirror and checked his new-found impact position. He compared his impact position to that of Hogan, Wright and Elkington. He looked identical to them now, at least without a ball. He understood now why the best players look similar at impact, hitting the ball with the center of the clubface. That way the loft of the club got the ball into the air. The clubface positions of the players were now apparent to J.B. He had never noticed this before, but after the last lesson, it was crystal clear. The information was coming in small, understandable pieces. However, he was still playing badly. The scores had gotten only a little better, and that was because of better putting. He now hit shots *solidly* into water hazards and out of bounds. That was certainly going to be a topic of conversation in today's lesson. J.B. walked out to the tee.

"Good afternoon, Coach. How're you doin'?" asked J.B.

"I'm doing great. How did it go for you the last two weeks?"

"My mechanics are coming along great, and I'm hitting the ball a lot more solid, but I played last Saturday and . . . it wasn't any fun," J.B. said, disappointment edging his words.

"That's to be expected, unfortunately. If I were giving you piano lessons, I wouldn't have had you in a recital yet," Harry said with a broad smile.

"I hadn't thought of it that way. Should I not play right now?"

"Oh, it's fine to play. You just need to have realistic expectations on the golf course. You have old, bad habits competing against new, good ones. Sometimes the old ones win out and sometimes it's a garbled mess of both. Here's the part where patience and faith play a big part. Patience, so that you give yourself enough time, and faith in your instructor that he or she is telling you the right things."

"I do have those, but I just want to beat those guys and have 'em eat their words," said J.B.

"I can assure you that if you keep doing the things we talk about each lesson, you will beat those guys, and they will be eating crow. . . . Probably taking lessons themselves," Harry added.

J.B. and Harry shared a laugh.

"Now, let's get to it, J.B. Let me see you chip some for me."

J.B. pulled out a wedge and chipped some just off the edge of the tee. His wrists were solid, with only a hint of the flippiness of the past. His weight was very firmly on his left side.

"A quote I picked up years back from the great Master's champion and club pro, Claude Harmon: 'Your left wrist should be like Bethlehem Steel—no linguine'," Harry said, as he held the club in his left hand with a bowed wrist and showed J.B. what he meant by "Bethlehem Steel."

"You have made great progress since our last lesson, but you could exaggerate a bit more," Harry continued. "Today in the short game portion of our lesson, I'm going to show you how to pitch the ball. This has added significance because the full swing is a glorified pitch shot. All the elements of a full swing, except for the length of swing, are included in a pitch. One of the main differences between a chip and a pitch is that with the pitch we are hitting longer, lofted shots, which requires the hinging of the wrist. So, today let's work on the wrist hinge. Go ahead and take that wedge back to hip high," Harry instructed.

J.B. took the club back, though he wasn't sure if it was where Harry wanted it.

"Let me show you how to take the club back," said Harry. He grabbed J.B.'s shoulders and turned them, at the same time placing his club and arms in position, with his wrists hinged.

J.B.'s hands were even with his belt buckle, and if a laser beam had been coming out of the butt of the club, it would have pointed to the target line.

"I just moved you through a correct start of the swing. This has been extremely misunderstood through the years, because in an attempt to keep something simple that's not simple, we have seen misconceptions abound. Telling someone to take the club 'straight back and straight through' has led to steep backswings and out-to-in forwardswings. 'Keep the head still,' in combination with 'straight back and straight through,' has led to pivots where the weight is on the left foot in the backswing and on the right foot in the forwardswing, which we call a reverse pivot. 'Let the wrists hinge naturally' is very vague and has led to a floppy wrist hinge at the top with no control over the clubface. This is another reason a person needs a qualified teacher, because this is easier shown than explained. By moving you into the correct spot, I accomplish four or five things that would be very difficult to explain," said Harry as he moved J.B. into this correct spot again and again.

"Let me show the wrong backswing moves." He moved J.B.'s left shoulder down and right shoulder up; the weight was on the left side. "This is a tilt of the shoulders that leads to a reverse pivot, and this is the excessive upper body movement to the right that I call a sway." Harry moved his head past his right foot." He then showed J.B. the two most common takeaway faults: first, arms and club way inside the target line and second, straight back along the target line and up. "These two directions are what I call off-plane. I'll explain on-plane to you in the second half of the lesson. Let's hit some shots with the correct backswing I showed you," said Harry.

J.B. took the club back and Harry made a small adjustment to his shoulder turn. J.B.'s wrists were hinged and his hands were at hip-high. He made a forwardswing, passed through the correct impact position and stopped with his hands at hip-high on the follow through.

Correct pivot

Sway

Reverse pivot

"This is a tilt of the shoulders that leads to a reverse pivot, and this is the excessive upper body movement to the right that I call a sway."

"Do that practice swing and brush the grass each time you do it. Notice where the clubface is," Harry said as J.B. lined up to the flag to which Harry had pointed.

J.B. began hitting shots that were solid, but still a little to the left. The backswing felt very different from his old one, which told him his old backswing was wrong. Since his lessons with Jack, he had moved his head and all of his weight to the right. He had tried to stop moving so much in the last couple of years, but it had become ingrained during those two lessons. This new backswing felt different, but it also felt more athletic. The shots were flying out with a similar flight. Harry came over and moved him through the correct movement a couple more times to get it ingrained. He also had him look in a mirror that was set up next to the teaching area.

"I can really see and feel the difference between my old backswing and my new one. How long do you think it will take to make it feel natural?" J.B. asked.

"You can't put a definite time on it, but it will take more than two weeks and less than six months. I know that's a broad answer, but habits are formed by doing something the same way repetitiously. We just need plenty of correct reps," Harry said.

"Am I doing it right?" J.B. asked, taking the club back and holding it there for Harry to check out.

"Yes, you are eighty percent correct. Just a couple of adjustments," Harry said. He moved the club a little bit and moved J.B.'s shoulders slightly. "Hit a few more shots."

The shot pattern was coming along nicely. "You are making such a nice pass at the ball now," Harry said encouragingly. Harry's eyes lit up, and he gave J.B. a pat on the back.

"Let's move to the second part of today's lesson, which is swing plane. Come over to my plane board," Harry said, waving J.B. toward a piece of plywood that had been cut in half and placed upright long ways with adjustable legs. A half moon notch was cut out of the middle of it, and it was covered with green Astro-turf. Harry stood where the notch was and spoke.

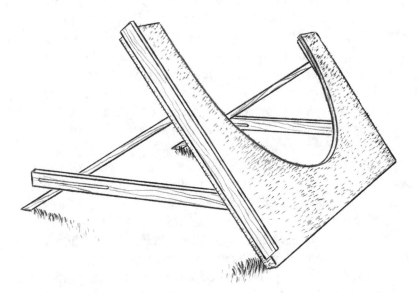

"Let's move to the second part of today's lesson, which is swing plane. Come over to my plane board . . ."

"The golf club is built with an angle between the clubface and the shaft. It is not built like a croquet mallet or a pool cue, which would go straight back and straight through. The angle that is created means the club is most efficiently moved or swung along a specific shape. The shape of the swing is what is known as swing plane. In geometry, a plane is a flat, thin surface. For example, a table top is on a horizontal plane"—Harry pointed to a table that he had outside—"and a door is on a vertical plane." Harry motioned up and down. "Swing plane is a tremendous concept that, once pictured in your mind, shapes the way you swing and gives you an understanding of path."

Harry stopped a moment, tilting his head to question whether J.B. was following. J.B. nodded, and Harry continued. "This is another concept that, in people's attempt to describe it simply, has actually hurt golfers' swings. 'Straight back and straight through' is an over-simplification that, as I said earlier, has led to vertical backswings and out-to-in forwardswings. 'Take the club inside' has led to swings that are too flat on the backswing and out-to-in on the forwardswing. There are also people who have made it too complicated by talking about exact degrees or angles. An overall picture of the shape and some key check points are what will help you develop an on-plane swing and get rid of that pull you've been hitting."

"I am definitely ready to get rid of the pull." J.B. pointed to his divots from earlier that were going left.

"One more piece of information that will sound technical at first but will make the checkpoints simple and understandable is what I call the law of swing plane. The low end of the club"—Harry pointed to the club head, then took the club half way back and pointed to the butt end of the club—"will point to the target line unless there is no low end"—Harry showed the club going parallel to the ground—"and there it will be parallel to the target line." Harry paused. "There, that wasn't so bad, was it?"

"No, but I'm counting on your moving me through it to make sure I grasp it." J.B. got into his posture, knowing the routine by this point.

"Hey, you're getting pretty good at the steps in learning. First comes the explanation and demonstration of concept, then comes the feel by moving you through some moves or check points. Remember in chipping, we did some toe up to toe up drills, and I told you that the club was parallel to the target line on the small backswing and follow through?"

"Yes," said J.B.

"I snuck swing plane in on you and you didn't even know it. Then today when we added the hinge to your pitch shot, remember that I told you a laser beam coming out of the club would point to the target line?"

"Yesss," J.B. said playfully, catching on to where Harry was going with his explanation.

"I snuck swing plane in on you again, so that I could teach it to you without ever telling you. But I think it helps in the long run for you to understand it. These check points let you know if you are too flat or too upright. So, let me ask you a question. Should the club go straight back or inside?"

"It should go gradually inside to the shaft parallel checkpoint you showed me," J.B. said, demonstrating.

"Good answer, and how about from there? Where do you go?"

"I would hinge the club so that a laser beam from the butt end of the club would point to the target line."

"Right again. How about from there?" Harry asked, letting J.B. run with the idea.

"If the club got to parallel at the top, the club would be parallel to the target line. . . . Uhhh, from there you're going to have to help me because my downswing has been a problem."

"Okay!" Harry jumped in to show him. "As the club starts down, the arms will drop and the butt end will again point to the

Backswing

Forwardswing

"Swing plane is a tremendous concept that, once pictured in your mind, shapes the way you swing and gives you an understanding of path."

target line"—Harry moved J.B.'s arms down—"instead of starting down this way." Harry showed the too-familiar out-to-in plane.

"Yeah, I recognize that one. That's my over-the-top move," J.B. said.

"Once you approach the ball from the inside, then along the target line at impact with the face square, that will send the ball to the target instead of left." Harry paused as he moved J.B. through the correct movement so there was no misunderstanding. "Now, that wasn't so hard to understand, was it?"

"No. But having you move me through the positions so I can feel them makes all the difference in the world."

"Let me show you one other thing about using checkpoints. One thing I pride myself on is building swings that are fluid and seemingly without checkpoints. The checkpoints are to check the direction and shape of your fluid swing. They are not to be overdone into a robotic, stiff movement. So, make sure as you practice to spend as much time flowing through the positions as you do stopping to look at your checkpoints."

"I have one more question," J.B. said.

"Shoot!"

"What about unorthodox swings, like those of Jim Furyk, Miller Barber, Lee Trevino and Ray Floyd? Don't they violate swing plane?"

"First, let me tell you that I love unorthodox swings that work, as they do for the players you mentioned. The first criterion of my teaching is results. If you came to me with good results, I wouldn't change you. These players are very orthodox where it counts: on the forwardswing as they approach impact. So, they don't violate swing plane and path on the forwardswing. That's how they are different from the players who say 'my swing's unorthodox like Lee Trevino's. I just need to practice more.' In most cases, these players are out-to-in with poor impact, and they don't have any face control. They use this as an excuse not to change, so they don't get better. You don't have to have an on-plane backswing to be a good ball striker, but it doesn't hurt."

"I think I would prefer an on-plane backswing and forwardswing. It just seems to me that it would be simpler." J.B. proclaimed.

"I'm glad you feel that way. Let's hit some balls with your new and improved swing plane."

J.B. started hitting a few shots. The first one was actually a shot off the hosel of the club, but the shots that followed encouraged J.B. When he let his arms feel as though they dropped and also seemed to be swinging out to the right, he hit some shots that actually went to the target. He felt as though his divots would go to the right, but they actually went to the target instead of left. Harry quickly videotaped J.B.'s swing from behind, so he could see the difference between his out-to-in swing and the new feeling. They looked at the swing together.

"First, let me show you your old swing," Harry said, rolling the tape. J.B. could see the distinct out-to-in movement. "Now, let me show you the new feeling." Again Harry rolled the tape and J.B. could see the difference, but it wasn't really as different as it felt.

"I can't believe that. It feels so much more exaggerated," said J.B.

"That's the difference between fact and feel, and it's exactly the reason I use video analysis. I pick only one or two key things to look at to avoid giving the student 'paralysis by analysis'. One of the biggest barriers to your getting better is the gap between what you *feel* you're doing and what you are *actually* doing. When I show you this on video, we can see what principles to focus on, and you can see how much you need to exaggerate. It would be very difficult to do this on certain swing faults without a video camera."

"I can see that I should feel more drop in the arms and more in-to-out to get me on-plane."

"That's right, and it would be natural for you to have your doubts without videotape. Let me see a couple more."

J.B. was determined to exaggerate even more. He actually had one shot start right of the target and draw back to the left.

"Hey, there it is! My first draw shot. I've never hit a draw shot before." J.B.'s smile nearly split his face.

"I told you. There's no slicing on this lesson tee," Harry said with a smile equal to J.B.'s. "We're going to have to wrap it up today. Use your drills and checkpoints, and don't forget about our earlier lessons. Do some putting and chipping, and work on your pre-swing. I'll see you again in two weeks if that works into your schedule."

"It does!"

"Do you have any questions?"

"No. I beleive I understand what we worked on. Thanks for the help."

"You're welcome. Just keep doing a little bit every day, and your improvement is guaranteed. We'll introduce pivot in the full swing and distance control in the short game next time."

"Sounds great. I'll make those guys eat their words in no time."

"No doubt about it," said Harry. They shook hands and Harry cleaned up a bit around the studio. J.B. practiced a while longer and went home thinking about his progress.

9
As the Body Turns

LESSON DAY AGAIN. The preceding two weeks had presented the usual problems at work and at home. His one round of golf had again been dissatisfying. Inconsistency in direction was the problem. He would hit one to the left, and the next he would leave out to the right. Army golf they called it—left-right, left-right. Though he knew what to do, his old habits were still too strong. They were like a wild bronco that couldn't be broken. It was going to take time. His practice time was limited, but focused. He knew his drills and had a pretty good idea about when he was getting it right. He worked on his putting mat for 15 minutes each morning. His stroke was becoming quite simple, and he had learned to line up well.

J.B. ate breakfast and got to Fox Run just after ten. He wanted to practice lag putting and chipping, because Harry was going to work on distance control with him. The distance and touch in his putting were getting better, but his chipping was another story. He hit them all solidly now, but most went too far. When he tried to hit the shot softer, he would decelerate and mis-hit it. Today was definitely a good time to work on touch. After the short game tune-up, he went to the studio to check his movements in the mirror and hit a few warm up balls before the lesson.

Harry liked having his students use the practice area. He had specifically developed it and set it up so that it would support the learner before, during and after the lesson. These included mirrors for feedback, training aids that were used during the lessons, and specific situations set up around the short game area. This was a place very conducive to learning.

J.B.'s posture looked right in the mirror, and it didn't feel strange any more. His backswing and forwardswing were on plane, at least when he wasn't hitting a ball. He went out to the plane board and swung back and forth along the board. It still felt as though his backswing was more to the inside and his forwardswing dropped, but the club was on the board, so, in reality, there was no loop. He checked his clubface positions, which were also becoming second nature. He could feel where the clubface was without looking. He thought to himself, *It sure takes some work, but I'm getting this*. He went down to the left side of the tee where the tree was, to try to curve right-to-left shots around it. His new nemesis, the pull shot, reared its ugly head. The first couple pulled left into the tree. J.B. remembered that on video from the last lesson he could exaggerate more, so he swung the club way in-to-out. His shot just barely missed the branches of the large pine tree, and the ball curved to the left. *That shot will come in handy one of these days*, he said to himself. It was almost 11:00 and time for his lesson. A glance to his right told J.B. that Harry's 10:00 lesson seemed to be coming along fine.

"Are you warmed up and stretched out?" Harry called out from across the tee.

"I still need to stretch!" J.B. yelled, a little embarrassed.

Harry flashed J.B. a look that said, *Get it done*.

J.B. went through his stretching routine, then came up to the lesson area.

"Let me see some pitch shots to that yellow flag," Harry said, pointing toward the familiar flag.

J.B.'s shots were crisp. As Harry observed J.B.'s swing, J.B. sensed the pleasure his teacher felt in seeing his student's athletic posture, the better swing plane, and the excellent impact. There were still things to work on, but J.B. knew he was coming along nicely; he could see it in Coach's face.

"We're going to work on your full swing pivot today. The pivot is the way your body moves in the swing." Harry made a backswing as he spoke. "It all starts in your posture, which you are doing very well. I actually got you started on this last time when I moved your shoulders the correct way and the wrong way. Remember, I defined 'secondary angle' for you? Well, it will be easier for me to say secondary angle than 'slight tilt back' every time. This angle and the forward bend from your hips are the angles around which your body rotates. As I told you with swing plane, I could do this without telling you by moving you the correct way, but I think in the long run it will help you better understand what you are doing. Now, I'm going to move your shoulders while we look in the mirror."

He stood behind J.B., facing the mirror. Harry moved J.B.'s shoulders the correct way, as well as his hips. When J.B. looked in the mirror he could see that the secondary angle was the same.

"The secondary angle becomes a great checkpoint," Harry continued. "Now, let's turn to the side and look." Looking at the down target line view, Harry turned J.B.'s shoulder and hips again.

From this angle J.B. could see that his shoulders turned around his spine. There was no raising up or tilting down.

"As I said to you in the last lesson," Harry went on, "this is a hard thing to explain. It is much easier to show you. Because of this, it's hard to learn pivot from a book. You need to experience it." Harry kept moving J.B. in the correct motion.

"What about weight shift?" J.B. asked. "I hear about this all the time, and Jack had me do a big weight shift."

"That's a good question. We hear and read about this a lot," Harry replied. "If it were as simple as just shifting back to the right side and then through to the left side, players wouldn't

Good secondary angle

No secondary angle

"The secondary angle becomes a great checkpoint . . ."

have as many problems as they do. There should be more weight on the right in the backswing and more weight on the left in the forwardswing and finish. At the same time, the body is turning and the arms are—we hope—swinging on plane. The weight shift is a piece of the puzzle, but not the whole puzzle." As he spoke, Harry moved J.B.'s shoulders and hips.

"Over all these years of teaching, I've found that moving you correctly while explaining some things is the best way to get you to feel it and do it correctly. I also think it leaves the least chance for misunderstanding."

As he spoke, Harry continued to move J.B.'s shoulders the correct way. "Back to my belief that one day golfers will perceive learning golf the same way as a person wanting to learn martial arts," Coach said with a smile. "I've toyed with the idea of having belts or medals to go along with the short game handicapping and full swing development. It would be another way of measuring progress and motivation."

Harry stopped tugging on J.B.'s shoulders and stepped back. "Let's see you hit a few short shots."

J.B.'s swings were a little awkward as he made this different movement.

"Hit a few more," Harry said. "I want to show you quickly on videotape what you are doing."

J.B. hit a few shots while Harry videotaped.

"Now, come here and look at this," said Harry as he got the videotape ready to show J.B. There was a hint of delight in Coach's voice.

"Wow, that is much better!" J.B. exclaimed. "I can see what you mean by secondary angle now. I'm turning instead of swaying." Together they looked at the screen. For J.B., the tape confirmed that, though it felt weird and different, it was correct. "Will this eventually feel normal?" he asked.

"Yes, just like the grip and posture now feel normal," Harry assured him. "Let's hit some more shots."

J.B. had to work at this change. He physically had to exert a force to keep his body from doing the old move to which it was accustomed.

"A couple more shots, J.B., and then we're going to move to the second half of the lesson, distance control."

"Sounds great," J.B. replied as he continued to hit shots.

"Let's go over to the green," Harry said. "Go ahead and bring your bag, because we're going to use a few different clubs."

J.B. grabbed his name-embossed bag and followed Harry.

"Grab your putter first of all," Coach said. "Let's hit some longer putts."

J.B. grabbed his Ram Zebra putter and a sleeve of golf balls.

"Some people say feel can't be taught," Harry said. "They say feel can only be learned. I guess this is true to an extent, but I can lead you through drills and ideas that will help you discover your feel. Whether this is teaching or learning or both, it really doesn't matter. First, let me see you hit a couple to that hole." He pointed to a hole roughly 30 feet away.

J.B. lined up and hit the three balls. One went long and two were short. One of the short ones was also three feet to the left. J.B. looked sheepishly at Harry. "I guess we've got some work to do, Coach."

"Yes, I guess we do," Harry replied as they walked over to pick up the balls. "Let me have you toss the balls over to this hole and see how close you can get them," Harry said, pointing to a different hole that was 30 to 35 feet away.

"Toss them like this?" J.B. mimicked a softball pitch.

"Yes, just like that."

J.B.'s first toss went too far. He then adjusted and the next two were pretty close.

"Now, let me ask you a question, J.B. How did you know how hard to toss the balls?"

"The first one was too hard, so the next two I tossed softer," replied J.B.

"That's right. Let me point out that you didn't change your mechanics and you didn't agonize over it. You just did it. Here's my point. I see a lot of golfers who get a putter in their hand and stand over the ball for an eternity attempting to get the speed perfect. What we need is the same process that you just did." Harry had a putter to demonstrate. "Assuming reasonable path, face and centered hits, you need to hit a putt and then adjust by feel." Harry hit a couple of putts. "The process to be avoided is trying to be perfect on every putt, which leads to tightness and a roadblock to your feel. Let the brain feel a long one and short one, and it will calculate the middle between the two."

"I do stand over my putts for a long time."

"That's your attempt to get it perfect and not mess up. Let's do a drill using your three balls. Using the principle we just talked about, hit the first putt long, the second putt short, and then split the difference for perfect speed. That gives your brain the information that it needs."

J.B. did the drill and, sure enough, by knowing how long and short felt, he was able to stroke the third putt and feel how hard to hit it. "I see what you mean!" J.B. exclaimed, a sense of "ah-ha!" in his voice. "It would be like throwing an out pattern in football. You lead the guy too much on the first throw and then maybe throw it behind him on the next. By then you've figured out the right amount to lead him on the third one."

"That's right. It's a process of trial and error and paying attention to the feeling that works. Another drill is hitting putts with your right hand only. This drill gets you to stroke the putt and not over-control it as we sometimes do with two hands. I've had many students who, to their surprise, were better with one hand than with two. Try a few," Harry urged.

J.B. followed Coach's command. The putts had a flow to them. His ability to hit the balls close without much thought or effort was surprising to J.B. "Why does this work?" he asked.

"I think it makes you more like the person throwing the ball. You look at the target and you throw it. Then you adjust, if necessary. There's no staring at the target with rigid arms as if that would somehow make you get it closer."

J.B. hit a couple more putts using this idea.

"I've got another good drill for you," Coach said. "In this drill you hit putts to a hole anywhere from 30 to 60 feet away. You can do this with a partner or by yourself. Once you hit the putt"—Harry demonstrated—"you don't look. Instead, think about how it felt and then call it out before you look. Did it feel left or right, short or long? Then you look to see how close you were to being correct. The closer this matches what you guessed, the better feel you have. Give it a try."

J.B. hit a putt to a hole 40 feet away.

"What do you think?" asked Harry.

"Short and left," J.B. called out. The put actually stopped right next to the hole.

"The right distance and the right direction!" announced Harry. "Now think about how that affects your putting. When you get ready to hit a putt, you look at the hole and then you look back at the ball. When you hit the putt, it is based on your perception and feel as to how far it goes. The closer you can match perception with reality, the better your touch is. Try it again." Harry motioned toward the hole.

Another putt was on its way.

"What do you think? " asked Harry.

"Long and left," J.B. said, then looked to see if he was correct. The putt was long and left.

"Hey, you're starting to feel it! Now let's try another drill." Harry took his putter and demonstrated a putt while looking at the hole instead of the ball. "When you're playing other sports, like basketball or baseball, you look at your target and then throw or shoot. You are responding to your target. This drill gets you to respond to your target by looking at it."

Harry motioned for J.B. to give it a try.

"I feel as though I can't hit the ball if I'm not looking at it," J.B. admitted.

"You might mis-hit a few at first, but once you get used to it, you'll sense where the ball is."

"This really feels weird not to look at the ball," J.B. said on the first few attempts, seeing that his balls were off on their distance, although they started to get better the more he did it. "I can get my speed better by looking at the target."

"The previous drill was feel through perception. This one is feel through vision. When you do these drills you are making your senses more attentive and tuned in. That's where touch and feel come from."

J.B. hit a few more. Each one finished within two feet of the hole.

"Unfortunately, we're running out of time for this lesson," Harry said. "You do similar drills for chipping, but I'll pick up on this at our next lesson. Will two weeks from now work?"

"That would be great," J.B. said, nodding.

"We're going to tie your swing movements together by having good rhythm and swinging the club at our next lesson," Coach said. "And we'll also continue on touch and distance control in your short game."

"Sounds like a winner. I appreciate your help once again. Harry, have a great July Fourth weekend."

"Thanks. And you keep making these things into habits." Harry slid into his cart and headed back to the clubhouse. J.B. continued to practice.

10

The Swing's the Thing

THE USUAL FOURSOME—J.B., BILL, BRIAN, AND ROBBY—had decided to play Ironwood for their customary Saturday contest. The summer heat and the long Fourth of July weekend, which usually brought out more golfers, had made an early morning round a must. J.B. knew he was getting close to a breakthrough round, and his confidence was growing.

"Bill, are you ready to put it on these guys today?" J.B. asked for the umpteenth time.

"I'll do my best," Bill answered with his normal lack of conviction. The bets were made and the familiar razzing took place. J.B. got off to his best start ever. Par, par, bogie on the first three holes.

"This won't hold up," Brian said after the third hole when he was one down. He was right. J.B. played the next three holes: bogie, double bogie, double bogie. Brian was now one up. As they arrived at the ninth hole, J.B. was two down, and he said the words Brian wanted to hear: "I press." All the tee shots were down the middle, with J.B.'s going the farthest. He had been outdriving Robby and Brian consistently for the first time. Nothing was said, but J.B. knew it was eating at them. Both Brian and J.B. missed the green to the left.

"Closest to the pin for a dollar," Brian proposed.

"You're on," J.B. responded, knowing his touch was better than it used to be.

Brian hit his shot first and it came up five feet short. "That's not my best effort, but it'll be close enough to beat you," Brian bragged.

"That was the old me. I can get it closer than that." J.B. set up and hit his shot. He had been practicing this shot for the past month. The shot rolled inside Brian's, three feet past the hole. "Pay up!" J.B. exclaimed, holding out his hand. Taking money from Brian couldn't wait till after the round.

"Even a blind squirrel finds a nut sometimes," Brian retorted as he paid.

They made their putts, with Brian winning the front side, but J.B. had the moral victory.

On the back nine, J.B. got off to another good start. He was starting to see his hard work pay off. He still made a lot of mistakes, but they were different now—no slices, no tops and only a few where he hit behind it. Brian was behind again.

"Don't worry. He'll choke," Brian said to Robby as they rode in the cart to the green on sixteen. Sure enough, J.B.'s success was more than his comfort zone could handle. He lost the last two holes, thus losing by one on the back.

"Close, but no cigar," Brian zinged.

"You know you're starting to sweat. It's just a matter of time," J.B. retorted.

"Yeah, J.B., you had him," Bill chimed in.

"His day is coming," J.B. stated confidently.

* * *

The now familiar 11:00 lesson time rolled around, with J.B. raring to go. The momentum was building with each lesson. Success in the various areas of his swing was giving him a burgeoning sense of confidence. No longer did he miss a shot and have absolutely no idea why. He knew why the ball curved and how to hit it solidly, and he understood the ideal pivot that would give him a solid base of operations and momentum for his swing. His short game had improved markedly. He was now able to save strokes during his round, instead of throwing them away. As Harry had told him, "Defense wins championships in football and basketball. Short game wins championships in golf." This statement came back to J.B. often as he practiced and as he watched his scores start to drop. He went through his stretching routine to get limber and be ready for the lesson.

"Good morning, J.B. Let's get down to business," Harry said as he motioned toward the balls set up in his lesson area. "Are you warmed up already?"

"Yeah. I've stretched and hit a few balls. I'm ready to go. Which club?" J.B. asked with his hand on his clubs.

"Grab your wedge and let me see a few pitch shots," Harry said.

J.B. grabbed his wedge, which had seen a lot of action lately in his practice sessions. As he hit shots 40 to 60 yards, J.B. could almost feel Harry's pride in having a pupil do well. The shots were crisp because of the great impact position J.B. had developed. The shape of his swing was very close to the swing plane Harry had described to him. J.B. had some small errors, but the large errors were gone. His pivot still needed some work, but Harry assured him it wouldn't be long before it was right where it should be.

"Good job, J.B. I can see that you practiced between lessons. That always makes your coach happy. Grab your seven-iron, and let's talk about swinging the club and rhythm."

J.B. switched clubs, rattling the ones in the bag as he pulled out a seven-iron.

"Rhythm is the repeating beat of your golf swing." Harry held a club suspended by his thumb and forefinger, swinging it back and forth. "Notice as the club swings, it has the same beat." Harry gave a smooth, even count in sync with the club movement, "one-two, one-two." Harry did this for a while to make his point. "Your swing beat needs to match up to the rhythm of this club. Tempo is the relative speed of the swing based on your personality. Fast people swing faster than slower, more laid-back people. I notice my students' personality and temperament and help them make a rhythmic swing within that personality." Harry continued to swing the club back and forth from his thumb and forefinger. "Quick, tension-filled swings are the norm in golf because of the desire to kill the ball and the lack of understanding of how to get distance."

"Yeah, when I think of swinging smoothly, like what you're talking about, I think I'm going to hit the ball really short," J.B. confirmed.

"I know. That's the perception that leads to the quick lunges at the golf ball. I call that hitting the ball with brute force instead of centrifugal force. The golfer tries to muscle the ball out to the target. It is, again, one of those instincts that has to be trained out of the golfer." Harry hit a shot that was long and true, yet effortless.

"Here's an equation for distance that I want you to remember. Clubhead speed plus centerface-hits equals distance. The ball does not know how fast the club is moving as you take it back. A ball responds to how fast the club is moving at impact. Also, you must hit the ball centerface to get maximum distance out of the club. With a rhythmic swing, the fastest moment is when the club is traveling through impact. That's the kind of efficiency we're looking for. Have you ever made a smooth swing and were completely surprised at how far it went?"

"Yes. In my last round I was trying to lay up in front of the pond on number six here at Fox Run. I made a smooth swing, and the ball went fifteen yards farther than normal . . . right into the pond."

"You accidentally stumbled upon rhythm and centrifugal force." Harry grabbed a thick string that had a ball attached to it. "This is a training aid that is similar to the one Ernest Jones showed in his book, *Swing the Clubhead*. He used a handkerchief and a penknife, and I use a string with a ball on the end. If you swing it back and forth"—Harry swung it from his thumb and forefinger like a club—"it is smooth and rhythmic. If you start jerking it around"—Harry exaggerated a jerking movement with the ball hitting him several times—"the resulting movement is erratic, at best." He laughed, rubbing a place the ball had hit, pretending to be hurt.

"The clubhead is a weight at the end of your shaft," he continued. "The erratic movement of the club is not as apparent as when I demonstrate with the ball and string, but it is just as damaging. When people develop a smooth, rhythmic *swing*, they have centrifugal force and physics working for them. This helps the player get repeatable results. Let me see you swing the club."

"All right." J.B. made a smooth swing that felt slow to him. To his surprise, the ball jumped off the clubface. The swing had felt effortless, but the ball flew longer. "I just can't believe I can swing that smoothly and hit the ball that far!" he exclaimed.

"It is an amazing thing," Harry agreed. "Our instinct tells us to kill it and muscle it. We have to learn to swing the club and have a well-timed acceleration of the club. Let me see you hit a few more, while feeling as though you're swinging at half-speed."

"Half-speed? Do you want me to make a full swing?" J.B. inquired.

"Yes. Full swing, half-speed."

J.B. hit a shot that felt very solid.

"Did that feel half-speed to you?" Harry asked.

"Yes, it did."

"It looked to me as though you were swinging at ninety percent. I want you to use that feeling on all your full swing shots for a while."

"Really? I don't know if I can trust swinging that slowly."

"Trust me. You'll be able to trust it because you are going to hit it so much more consistently. I've had students that swing so hard I had to get them to feel as though they were swinging at twenty percent or less to get them to have a rhythmic swing. . . . Make a few more swings."

J.B. hit a couple more shots that were solid, long and straight. He had never been able to get himself to swing the club effortlessly. He had always muscled the ball with a very tight grip. He had been told to swing smoother, and he had read that he should swing smoother, but he had not been able to do it. This was another real breakthrough. As he thought about it, these lessons had been a series of breakthroughs.

"Good job, J.B. What a good group of swings those were. You're going to play some very good golf in the near future. Those guys you play with had better watch out."

J.B. could see that Harry was as excited about his student's progress as he was. The coach did not try to disguise his pleasure.

"Those shots felt great. I just can't believe it," J.B. said.

"Let me tape you so you can see how fast it actually looks." Harry grabbed his camera and J.B. hit a few more shots. They went over to the portable monitor and deck that he had set up on the range.

"Watch this," Harry commanded.

J.B. peered at the monitor, which was set up at an angle to avoid the glare of the sun. "Wow! I can't believe that. I thought I was swinging at half speed, but it looks like full speed. I don't even want to know what I looked like when I was swinging hard."

"You're right. You don't want to see that. It isn't pretty," Harry joked. "Just remind yourself of this video when you start swinging harder."

"This feels a lot better."

"It's time to work on distance control. Let's go over to the short game area." Harry already had balls set up for chipping. "Grab your nine-iron to start."

J.B. pulled the nine-iron out as the other clubs clattered.

"First let me have you hit some chips to the hole." Harry pointed to a hole 50 feet away.

J.B.'s chips were solid, whereas a couple of months ago he couldn't get the ball on the clubface. Of the five he chipped, two were close to the hole and the other three were long.

"Distance control and touch start with solid contact. That's why I wait until now to work on this with you. Three months ago it would have done us no good because of your scooping. Now the ball comes off the loft at the same height each time and has a consistent roll. Your brain processes this new, good information and develops touch and feel."

J.B. hit a couple more chips that went past the hole. "I've noticed that my shots tend to go long, now," J.B. commented.

"That's a sign of solid contact. Now, I'm going to lay three clubs on the green about three feet apart, starting at five feet from the fringe." Harry laid the clubs down to the side of where J.B.'s balls were landing. "On the next few shots I want you to pay attention to where the balls land and then roll. These clubs will give us a reference."

J.B.'s first chip landed at the third club and rolled ten feet past the hole.

"Land this next one shorter."

This shot landed by the third shaft again and went twelve feet past. "I tried. I guess that's why we're working on my touch." J.B. laughed.

"That's right. Try again."

This shot landed at the first club and ended up five feet short.

"One more," Harry prompted.

This one landed at the second club and rolled the perfect distance. It was even with the hole and two feet left.

"That's where the ball needs to land for that club," Harry said. "Now grab your seven-iron."

Again the clubs clanked as J.B. grabbed the seven-iron and laid the nine-iron against his bag. "Obviously, I want to land this one near the first club," J.B. said.

"Exactly. Hit a couple with the seven-iron," Harry replied.

J.B.'s first landed just past the second club and rolled 15 feet past the hole. The next one landed at the first club and almost went in.

"Your touch is getting better. You made the adjustment after only one shot. Now let me show you the ladder drill."

"What's that?"

"I'm going to have you hit to the fringe of the green, which is about sixty feet away." Harry pointed to the spot. "You need to get as close to the fringe as you can without getting to it. Each succeeding ball needs to get as close to the previous ball without touching it or going past. You want to see how many balls you can get between the fringe and the stopping line, which I will put twenty feet from you. Let's give it a try."

J.B.'s first shot went onto the fringe.

"You lose. Start again," Harry prodded.

This time J.B.'s ball stopped about three feet away. "Hey, at least I got started this time," he joked. The next ball was short, and the next one rolled too far. "Well, I can see a drill that I'm going to be practicing these next two weeks," J.B. said.

"This will help you make each shot matter as you practice," Harry said. "That brings us to a good point about practicing. Your practice time should be split between technique practice and competition practice. A lot of people will hit a bucket of balls and think they have practiced. That would be technique practice, but you don't hit twenty six-irons in a row on the golf course. You get one shot, and they all count. So, part of your practice should be competitive or game simulation practice. This is where each shot matters. Competing against a friend in a putting or chipping contest. Chipping and then having to putt out. Hitting different clubs as if you were playing a course in your imagination. These are examples of simulating a golf situation so that you are preparing yourself for game day."

"I've never thought of doing that. I've always hit a bucket of balls, hit a few putts and called that practice."

"That's pretty typical. With the ideas of practice that I just presented to you, you can use your imagination to make up games that simulate playing situations."

"That makes a lot of sense. I was always trying to hit the ball better, so I hit a bucket of balls. I should have been practicing mechanics and real situations."

"Ah-ha! I knew you were a quick learner. Try the ladder drill one more time."

This time J.B. made it to five balls before he hit the sixth one past.

"Your technique is simple and effective, and your touch is starting to improve." Harry declared. "At the next lesson in two weeks, I'm going to have you come an hour early and take that skills test again."

"Good. I know I can do better than I did last time."

"I know you can, too, and we're going to measure exactly how much," Harry said.

"One more question, Coach. When do you look at my bunker play? It's the worst part of my game."

"The next lesson. I save it until later for a reason I'll tell you about in two weeks. Practice up for that skills test." Harry grabbed J.B.'s shoulder in a friendly gesture. "Do you have any more questions?"

"I always have more questions, but I'll save them for another time."

"Okay, I'll see you in two weeks. Keep up the good work."

11
The Match

J.B. OPENED HIS TRUNK to let one of Fox Run's bag drop guys grab his clubs.

"How are you this morning, Mr. Hawkins?"

"Fine, Bobby, how are you?"

"Could it be any nicer today?" Bobby asked.

"I can't see how." J.B. smiled.

"The rest of your group are already down on the range, warming up. I'll get you loaded up while you're checkin' in." J.B. thanked Bobby and gave him his usual tip. It never ceased to amaze him how nice and professional the Fox Run staff was.

Even before talking to Bobby, J.B. was in great spirits. Something felt different today. He had never beaten Brian, but he had gotten close lately. J.B. could feel it today. He couldn't quite put his finger on it, but he did feel the complete opposite of the way he used to at the course.

Bill and Robby were putting a few near the first tee, getting ready for the round. J.B. began warming up, confidence at the front of his mind set. It was obvious to him that his demeanor did not go unnoticed. He could feel Brian looking across the large putting green at him as he made quite a few six-footers in a row. These men were best friends, but on Saturdays there was a suspension of the friendship for four hours. Brian had become more and more serious about their Saturday rounds, even to the point of gamesmanship.

"Hey Robby, look at J.B. warming up! He's really got his game face on today," Brian blared from across the green.

"Sure does. I guess he thinks if he stares at the ball, he can will it in today," Robby retorted with a hearty chuckle.

"You guys sound nervous. Bill, are you ready to hurt these guys today?" J.B. volleyed back.

"Ready as I'll ever be," Bill said, but he didn't sound very confident. "I just need to get some breaks today."

"The Ahrens foursome is on deck. Please report to the tee," bellowed the starter over Fox Run's PA system. When they got to their carts, they rustled around to get gloves and balls and grab their drivers for the first tee shot. They had to go only 40 feet to get to the first tee from the putting green. The first hole was a simple, 390-yard par four with a wide-open fairway. It was probably the flattest hole on the golf course, which had a lot of hilly terrain.

Brian took the opportunity on the first tee to begin his mental dismantling of his good friend. "Putting stroke looked good on the practice green. Too bad it's not the same as playing under pressure," Brian crowed.

"Did you really like that stroke, Bry?"

"Yeah."

"Well you're going to be seeing those same results all day long," J.B. fired back.

"What's the game today?" Brian asked.

"We've got a two-dollar Nassau for the teams, and you and I have our usual," J.B. answered.

"You want to raise the ante a little bit for our game?" Brian proposed.

"Absolutely! You name it," J.B. shot back.

"Five-dollar Nassau with dollar birdies."

"It's your funeral," J.B. said. "You're mine, today!"

"Not gonna happen." Brian did his best impression of Dana Carvey doing George Bush.

"Hey, are we gonna have to separate you two?" Bill asked, laughing. The ceremonial flip of the tee confirmed that J.B. and Bill were up first.

"Well, we might as well give them the tee on one hole today," Robby said, elbowing Brian.

"You lead us off, Bill," J.B. said.

Bill took out a tee and put his ball on it.

"Watch out for that trouble down the left side," Robby playfully needled.

Bill was a slicer, and he hit his customary banana ball that finished down the middle.

"Okay, J.B. Let's see the best swing that money can buy," Brian chortled.

"Believe me buddy, you're gonna get sick of seeing it," J.B. countered. J.B. was now hitting a draw, but the pull could still jump up and get him. With the nerves of the first tee shot, that's exactly what happened. Luckily for J.B., it was a wide-open hole.

"You better keep that under control today. There's a lot of trouble on the left side at this golf course," Brian reminded him. Brian and Robby's tee shots were playable, and the round was under way.

As Brian said, J.B. did, indeed, have on his game face. It took plenty of concentration to do his new, improved swing and not fall back into his old habits. An added dimension today was his feeling, for the first time, that he could beat Brian. The first hole was halved with bogies. J.B. and Bill won the second hole with J.B.'s up and down par from the rough, to put them one up, and it put J.B. one up on Brian. The match was nip and tuck and all even as they arrived for the ninth hole. This was a 440-yard par four that had humbled many a golfer. Bill's tee shot had sliced too far to the right, with the other three down the middle.

J.B. and Brian had the same score going into the hole, and they were a lot more tight-lipped than at the beginning of the round. Brian was up first, and for the first time that J.B. could remember, both the match and Brian's tongue were tied. He hit his approach shot fat, and it came up short. J.B. knew he had an opening to beat Brian on this nine. He selected his club, went through his routine, and hit the shot. He had done it again. His new mistake, the pull. He had swung out-to-in and hit the ball over to the left side of the green. He was near the bunker, but not in it. J.B. breathed a sigh of relief. He still didn't know how to deal with bunkers. J.B. and Brian weren't really aware of Bill and Robby at this point. They were in their own little battle. Brian chipped up to about eight feet, and J.B. chipped it past the hole by 10 feet.

J.B. was the first to putt.

"Hey J.B., go ahead and get that one close," Brian called out as J.B. stood over the ball.

J.B.'s concentration stayed on track, and his now simple, effective stroke rolled the ball right into the hole.

"Yes!" J.B. yelled as he raised his putter into the air. "Is that close enough for you?"

Brian didn't have a comeback for that one. He lined up over his putt knowing that if he missed, it would be the first time J.B. had beaten him for nine holes. His putt had a tiny break from left-to-right. Brian struck the putt, and it appeared that it would miss, but it broke harder than he had thought . . . right into the left edge of the hole.

"You thought you had me," Brian said as he pulled his ball out of the hole and pointed it at J.B. defiantly.

"I made you sweat on that nine. I'm gonna get you on the back," J.B. declared.

"In your dreams," Brian said, though he didn't sound very convinced.

They all grabbed a quick snack as they made the turn. The back nine at Fox Run was the tougher of the two. The match was still even as they arrived at the sixteenth hole. This one was a reachable par five that was 500 yards long, its last 100 yards up a steep hill. J.B.'s tee shot was the best of the day. He outdrove the other guys by 30 yards.

"Are you using one of those soft cover balls, Brian?" J.B. inquired with a devilish smile. He had gotten into a "zone" and was hitting the best shots of his life. After the other three had all laid up, J.B. was going for it. He had never reached this green.

"You're gonna give it a go, huh?" Bill asked his partner. "Are you sure? The match is tied."

"Yep. I can make it today," J.B. said with conviction.

"Don't hit it behind those trees on the left," Brian added.

"What trees on the left?" J.B. smiled. There was a sense of calm and confidence that he had never felt before on a golf course. He knew how to make this swing. He just knew it. All he had to do was execute. He stepped up to the ball with his three-wood and gave it a rhythmic pass. "Swing the club" had been his main swing thought all day. The shape of his swing was on plane, and it produced the on-target ball flight that had started to become customary for him. The ball sailed gloriously off the club. It flew high and straight. There was no hint of the old slice or the new pull. The ball took one bounce in front of the elevated green, rolled onto the green, and stopped 30 feet short of the back hole location.

Bill was more excited than J.B. He motioned to shake his hand, but wound up grabbing his shoulders and shaking him. Robby followed by giving J.B. a series of high-fives. When Brian came out of shock, he slapped J.B. on the back. "Great shot, buddy. I didn't know you had it in you," he said.

"I didn't either," J.B. admitted.

Brian's third shot buried in a greenside bunker. It took him two shots to get out and two putts for a seven on the hole. J.B.

lined up for his eagle effort with his hands shaking. He had never had an eagle, but this was becoming a round of firsts, so anything could happen. He hit the putt on a good line and the speed looked good. Bill and Robby had become his gallery and were heading for the hole to pull the ball out for him.

They stopped in their tracks and let out a disappointed "Awww," in unison, as they saw the putt turn an inch to the right at the hole.

J.B.'s head dropped. *Three feet from the hole. I was sure it was in!* he thought. He came up and tapped in for his birdie. "I guess I can take a tap-in birdie," J.B. said with tongue firmly in cheek.

"Yeah, I think so," Robby retorted.

They headed to the par three seventeenth. Both J.B. and Brian made bogies on the long 205-yard hole. As they headed to the eighteenth, J.B. was up by three strokes on the overall score and one up in the match. The eighteenth was a strong 425-yard finishing hole. J.B. was up first, and as he lined up the face to hit his shot, Brian said the magic words, "I press." J.B. had known it was coming.

"You got it," J.B. responded as he continued his routine. The tee shot was a carbon copy of the tee shot on sixteen. He was still in the "zone."

"Follow that," Bill chimed in for his partner.

"He's going to choke," Brian said as he readied himself for his own tee shot. His homemade swing produced a shot that flew down the left side in good position. Robby and Bill hit their drives in play, but they were clearly along for the ride as J.B. and Brian battled it out. Brian was up first and put the pressure on by hitting a six-iron within 25 feet of the back right hole location.

J.B. had blocked out as much of the situation as he could, but he had an adrenaline rush that left him tingling from head to toe. He regained his composure by picturing Coach standing there giving him the advice to "focus on the task at hand and enjoy the moment." He was unsure what to hit. Three months ago, 155 yards was a six-iron; for the past two weeks, a seven-iron would have been the choice. Right now, however, with this adrenaline, it might be an eight-iron. He took the eight-iron, because he knew he couldn't swing easy under the circumstances.

"You know what this is for, don't you?" Brian's gamesmanship continued.

"Yeah, it's to put you out of your misery," J.B. said as he stood behind the ball, looking at the flag. J.B. stepped up, put the club behind, waggled and pulled the trigger. He hit the ball solidly, but with an ever so slight pull. His ball hit the green and was 30 feet left of the hole just outside Brian's ball.

Bill was J.B.'s cheerleader as they rode to the green. "You can do it partner! We can finally beat these guys," Bill said, his voice just above a whisper.

The foursome arrived at the green as Brian continued his verbal assault. "How many three-putts have you had today?"

"None."

"Now's as good a time as any to experience it."

"I think I'll experience it some other time," J.B. fired back. He hoped his practice on touch with Harry would pay off now. He looked from a couple of different angles and decided on where to play it. With his putter aimed six inches outside the hole to the left, he made the stroke and started the ball rolling toward the hole. It stopped a foot short of the hole, and J.B. tapped it in for his four. An 83, his best score ever!

Brian could still win the press with a birdie. He gave it a bold roll . . . a little too bold. As it was rolling past the hole, Brian was yelling for it to stop. The ball didn't listen very well, stopping five feet past the hole. Brian looked over to see if J.B. would give him the putt, but J.B. just gave a little smile. Brian made the putt for par and an 86. J.B. had won the back nine and the overall, and had beaten Brian by three.

What a great feeling, J.B. thought.

"Great round, J.B.," Robby said with a hearty handshake.

"Hey, way to go partner! I hope I wasn't too heavy today," Bill added with a high five.

"You were the better man today. I'm coming to get you next time," Brian said with a tight-lipped smile. The foursome headed out to the parking lot.

"Are we going inside?" Bill asked.

"I can go in for a minute, but I can't stay long. I've gotta go somewhere to spend Brian's money," J.B. responded.

"Ha, ha. Very funny. I'll go in for a minute under protest," Brian said with a sneer, handing J.B. his winnings. Inside, the stories flowed, and J.B. gloated only a little.

* * *

J.B. arrived at Fox Run by 9:00, chomping at the bit. His victory over Brian the week before was still fresh, and he was pumped about his game. The week's practice had been very focused in getting ready for the short game test. J.B. putted and chipped at Fox Run's large putting green. The touch that had been nonexistent just three months before was now allowing him to hit shots close to the hole with regularity. A few of J.B.'s acquaintances at the facility complimented him on his noticeable improvement, and he thanked them for their comments. His usual ride to the back of the range was filled with thoughts of anticipation and praise for his proud Coach. As usual, Harry was busy with a lesson.

Lenny had the test set up and ready to go. "Are you ready for the test?" he asked.

"I'm warmed up and ready to go. Let's get to it," J.B. said enthusiastically.

"Good. Let's start with putting."

Lenny and J.B. headed to the green, with J.B. grabbing his putter.

"We'll do short putts first." Lenny had put down white paint dots at three, six, nine, 12 and 15 feet on two different holes. One hole was a right to left putt. The other was left to right.

J.B. putted two balls at each spot and kept track of the total number he made. That was then multiplied times two for the total score. The first time, J.B. had scored ten points by making five putts.

"Boom!" J.B. yelled as his tenth putt went in. "I doubled my score from last time!"

"Good job! That takes you from a 15-handicap to scratch on the short putts. Let's go to lag putting," Lenny said.

The lag putts were from 20, 30, 40, 50 and 60 feet to a hole that had three circles painted around it. One was a three-foot radius circle, the second was a six-foot and the third was a nine-foot radius. If the putt was made, it was worth three points. Inside the three foot circle was worth two points, inside the six foot circle was worth one point, inside the nine foot circle was worth zero points and outside the outer circle was minus one. J.B.'s touch was noticeably better. He actually made one of the putts on his way to 18 points.

"That's up from sixteen points last time," Lenny called out. "Good job! We'll do chipping next, and we'll go to the same hole as the lag putting."

"All right." J.B. went to get his nine-iron, which he was using a lot for chipping. At this station Lenny had J.B. hit five shots from a spot 60 feet away and five from 40 feet. J.B. tended to miss on the long side, but his chipping showed a marked improvement from his previous score of six. His score of 11 made him a 14-handicap.

"Let's go over to the bunker."

"Not what I've been looking forward to," J.B. admitted. "This is my worst category, and Harry hasn't worked with me on this yet. We're going to be in the bunker during today's lesson."

"I know. It's the worst category for most of our students when they start, but we'll make it a strong point over time," Lenny declared.

With a feeling of dread, J.B. stepped into the bunker. The scoring system was the same as for the lag putting, except the circles were five feet, 10 feet and 15 feet. J.B.'s phobia didn't help his results. A couple of shots ended up in the circle and received points, but the bladed shots over the green and the shots that he hit fat and left in the bunker led to a score of zero.

"Well, that's an improvement over the minus four that you had last time, but you'll learn a lot today."

"I'm ready for the bunker lesson," J.B. said with exasperation. "What's the next category?"

"Short pitches to the same hole as the bunker."

J.B. went to the designated spot that required him to carry the ball higher and farther than the chip shot. As with his chipping, J.B. hit his shots solidly and was missing past the hole. His score was a few points less than in the earlier test.

"Okay. The last category is the distance wedges," Lenny said. He led J.B. to the left side of the range near the tree they used for students to practice curving shots. For targets, they used a set of barrels that were 20 yards apart.

"In the barrel is worth three points. Zero to ten feet from the target is worth two points. Ten to twenty feet is worth one. Twenty to thirty feet is worth zero points and outside of thirty feet is a minus one," Lenny reminded J.B.

Two shots were hit to each target, and the score was recorded based on where the ball landed. J.B.'s shots were hit in the sweet spot of the club, and some went farther than he expected. This was his second worst category in the earlier test. His score was an eight instead of his earlier score of one.

"Way to go, J.B.!" Lenny shouted as he walked back from the hundred-yard barrel. "Let's total this up." Lenny added the scores and gave J.B. the results. "In three months you have gone from a twenty-one-handicap short game to a twelve-handicap, with a score of sixty-four. If it weren't for the bunker pulling you down, you would have been an eight-handicap." Lenny extended his hand. "Congratulations! Your hard work has paid off."

"Thanks, Lenny." J.B. gave Lenny a hearty handshake. "I knew it was going to be better, but I didn't know it would be this much. This makes me want to practice even harder."

"It's time for your lesson. Have fun." Lenny headed toward his student who was scheduled at eleven o'clock.

J.B. marched over to Harry and proudly handed him the results, saying, "Check this out."

"Great job, J.B.!" Harry patted J.B. on the back. "I guess you're ready for the bunker lesson."

"You've got that right." J.B. grabbed his sand wedge and they headed for the bunker. This was the thing J.B. avoided most during a round of golf. He went over the green a lot of times to avoid a bunker that was guarding the front of the green.

"First, J.B., do you understand the design of a sand wedge?" Harry inquired.

"I think it has more loft. But other than that, I don't know," J.B. confessed.

"Before 1932, bunker shots were hit with a niblick, which is equivalent to a nine-iron or wedge. Have you heard of Gene Sarazen?"

"Yes. He was a great player in the era of Bobby Jones and Walter Hagen. I've also seen Master's highlights of him being the honorary starter off the first tee."

"That's right. As the story goes, he was taking a flying lesson and noticed that when the flap went down, the plane went up. This gave him an idea. He decided to put some solder on the back of a niblick. Instead of the club digging into the sand, it would now skid through the sand. This allowed the player to hit behind the ball into the sand, and the explosion of sand would propel the ball out. When Gene Sarazen went to the 1932 British Open, he kept the club turned upside down in his bag before the tournament began, so the ruling body would not have the chance to declare it illegal. He went on to win the tournament."

Harry held up a sand wedge and pitching wedge to show the difference between the two. "The sand wedge is designed with a flange that keeps the club from digging. The pitching wedge will dig, because it doesn't have the bouncing effect of the flange."

J.B. interrupted. "At this point, let me ask you a question. It sounds as though the club design should make hitting a sand shot pretty easy. And I've heard tour players say, 'It's the easiest shot in golf. You don't even hit the ball!' If it's the easiest shot in golf and it's my worst shot, does it mean I should take up another sport?" J.B. asked with a hint of sarcasm.

"That's a great question. I've been asked that many times over the years. I give lessons to the people for whom it is *not* 'the easiest shot in golf.' Here's the thing that the tour player doesn't understand. He can hit the sand he's looking at, just as he hits the ball first on a fairway shot. The average golfer hits behind the ball and sometimes tops it, while looking at the ball. This doesn't change in the bunker. If you can't hit your spot, you can't be a consistent bunker player," Harry finished with emphasis.

"So now that I can hit the ball fairly solid on my normal shots, should I be able to hit good bunker shots?" J.B. questioned.

"Exactly! So let's get to it. I bet you've heard that you should line up left, open the face and swing out-to-in."

"That's exactly what I've heard . . . and read, for that matter."

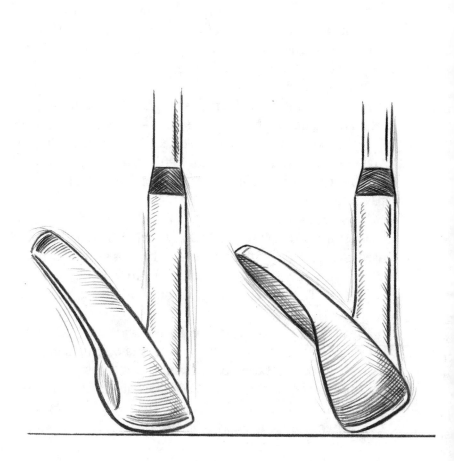

"The sand wedge is designed with a flange that keeps the club from digging."

"Well, there's some truth to that, but it's another over-simplification that gets people in trouble. Let me ask you a couple more questions. Why do you think the golfer should open the face for a bunker shot?"

"I would think to hit it higher."

"That's true. It would hit the ball higher, but that's not all it does. The flange, or bounce, increases"—Harry held up a sand wedge to show J.B.—"which would keep the club from digging even more. But what if you are in hard or wet sand?"

"The club would bounce into the ball and skull it," J.B. answered.

"That's exactly right. So instead of thinking that the club automatically should be open for every bunker shot, it's actually based on the texture of the sand and the type of shot that you're hitting. Now why should the path be out-to-in?"

"I would think that it's to compensate for the open clubface."

"That's right. But if you line up left *and* swing out-to-in, that would be too extreme." Harry demonstrated this steep, out-to-in swing. "If the texture of the sand is soft and you open the face for more bounce, you will line up slightly left, but make a normal swing," Harry again demonstrated with his usual flair. "Let me see you hit a couple of shots."

"If I must." J.B. set up left of the hole, took a mighty swing and . . . left the ball in the bunker.

"One more," Harry said.

This time J.B. made sure not to take so much sand, and he sent the ball sailing across the green. "That's how my bunker game is. If this is the easiest shot in golf, I should quit." J.B.'s disgust with himself came out.

"As I told you, it's not the easiest shot in golf. We need to get you to take the correct amount of sand. Also, the bottom of the divot should be under the ball. My favorite drill for this is the line drill." Harry took his club and drew a line in the sand.

"When you leave the ball in the bunker, you've either taken too much sand or hit too far behind it. When you skull the ball across the green, you have caught the ball first or, sometimes, the club has bounced into the ball."

"What does the line drill do?" J.B. inquired.

"If you can hit your spot and take a long, shallow divot, you will become a consistent bunker player. The line drill lets you see if you're doing that. Go ahead and hit the line."

J.B. stood with the line between his feet. He looked at the spot and tried to hit it. On the first attempt he actually hit four inches behind the line. The next was two inches in front.

"I thought this would be easy," J.B. exclaimed.

"There is no need to frustrate yourself hitting shots until you can hit the line consistently. When you hit the line consistently, you are on your way to being a good bunker player."

"Let me try it a few more times." J.B. continued to swing at the line. Each swing got closer and closer until he was hitting the line consistently.

"You see, J.B., I save bunker play until my players' impact has improved. When you're still scooping, you can't consistently hit your line. Your impact is good now, so it is just a matter of practicing the line drill until you do it consistently."

"Should I try a ball?"

"Yes." Harry moved a ball three inches in front of J.B.'s line. "Imagine that you are still doing the line drill and let the sand propel the ball out toward the hole."

J.B. hit about two inches behind his line and the ball barely got out of the bunker. "It got out, anyway!" J.B. exclaimed.

"That's right. Try it again," Harry exhorted.

This time J.B. hit his line, and the sand exploded the ball out, high and soft. "I can feel it! I just have to hit my line so that the sand knocks it out of the bunker, not my club hitting the ball."

Harry nodded in agreement, and J.B. continued to hit shots. Some were good and some mediocre, but he was getting better and gaining confidence with each shot.

"Harry, I can't believe it! I really thought I was just a bad bunker player and that I couldn't change."

"You *were* a bad bunker player. *Were* is the operative word there. By your skills getting better in earlier lessons and your understanding the concept of the sand wedge, you are going to improve quickly. You are actually going to get to where you like the bunker."

"That's hard to believe. But I can already see the progress. Hey, I've never hit shots out of the bunker like this before." The shots were coming out high and soft. J.B. looked down to see that he was hitting his line on all the good shots, and he was missing it on the poor ones. He realized the truth in Harry's saying that one skill builds to the next and the next and the next.

Harry watched J.B., with a smile on his face, continue to hit shots. "You didn't want to get in here to start the lesson, now you don't want to get out. But I want to spend the second half of the lesson working on your longer clubs."

"Okay, let's do it." When they arrived at the lesson area, Harry grabbed his video camera. "Let me see you hit some six-irons."

J.B. rattled around in his bag and pulled out the six-iron. He set up to the ball in a way that was balanced and athletic, and it felt normal. The shots were mainly solid, with a hint of a draw. The slice was long gone, but now he occasionally hooked the ball.

Harry taped these shots with the camera looking down the target line. "Hit the next couple of shots low," Harry requested as he moved the camera so he faced J.B.

His low shots were the most solid of all. They were lower now, and J.B. finished more on his left side.

"Come here and take a look."

Harry and J.B. moved to the monitor and Harry started the tape. They looked at his swing from the first view, down the target line. Harry paused the tape to show J.B.'s address position.

"What do you think?" Harry asked.

"I look like a tour player." J.B. was astonished.

"That's right. The posture, grip, and alignment that felt so bad three months ago now feel normal, and they are correct." Harry rolled the tape in slow motion and paused at the top. "Look at your clubface at the top. It's dead square."

The leading edge was in line with his forearm, where three months ago it was pointed down. "Once again, good job!" Harry said as he continued the tape in slow motion, pausing it just before impact. "I just want you to notice your right foot and knee. I'll point this out again from the other angle." He rolled the tape in slow motion to the finish. "So many things have improved. Let's look from the other angle." Harry fast-forwarded through three swings to get to the facing angle. "Your ball position is getting better." Harry had again paused at the set up. "Your secondary angle is also very good." He pointed to the small tilt of his upper body at address.

"I'm pleased with what I see," J.B. added.

"Great progress. I can get this kind of progress with anyone who will work with me long term and have trust during the times that it feels wrong." Harry rolled the tape again in slow motion. "I want you to notice your pivot. That's what we will work on today. You still move too far to the right with your upper body." The tape continued to roll without a pause until impact. "Look how much better your impact is. No wonder you're hitting the ball better. The handle of the club is forward as the ball is struck. The only thing that needs to change is that your weight needs to be more to your left side. Your right knee, hip and shoulder should be more forward to accommodate this." Harry demonstrated.

"I've practiced that. I thought I was doing it, but obviously I'm not doing it enough."

"That's where video helps. You can see it and practice what needs to be changed," Harry said.

"You know, I read an article that said video was bad, and that it caused 'paralysis'."

"When it's used incorrectly, it can. In those cases, the teachers—or people looking at it on their own—pick out too many things. This overload of information leads to the 'paralysis by analysis.' When used correctly, I don't know of a tool that has helped golf instruction more than the video camera and playback."

"What do you consider correct?" J.B. asked.

"When the instructor picks a priority, such as posture, and shows the student what is incorrect, and then changes him to a correct posture and shows him again. The new posture feels unusual and uncomfortable and it takes video or a mirror for the student to trust the change."

"I know it helped me. I would not have believed you about my posture and pivot until I saw it on videotape. It has helped me at each step."

"That's right. And you'll notice that I have only focused on one thing at a time with you so your attention didn't get diverted. I know I'm a broken record about this, but learning golf is about habit formation, not secrets, tips and gimmicks," Harry reiterated.

"I don't mind hearing you repeat it, because it has helped me a ton."

"Okay, let's work on your pivot some more." Harry shut off the camera and moved back toward the tee. As he had done in an earlier lesson, he moved J.B. into the correct turn, back and then forward, by moving his shoulders. He also had J.B. get to the top and then work on his forwardswing by moving J.B.'s knee, hip and shoulder more forward at impact.

This felt weird to J.B., but so had everything else. He knew to exaggerate and trust Harry. This went on for the remainder of the hour-lesson.

"Work on those feelings that we talked about, and I'll see you in two to four weeks. We covered the short game and full swing in a series of steps to educate you on the correct concepts. We got started on turning these things into habits. The lessons will follow a different pattern, now that your first six have been completed. I'll now be giving you feedback during each lesson on whether you are doing it right. Giving you the information is the teaching, and the feedback is the coaching. The future lessons will mainly be coaching."

"I'd still like to come back in two weeks to keep the momentum going. I also have some questions to ask you."

"Okay. Tell me this. How do you feel about golf now?"

"I love this game!"

Epilogue

THIS STORY INCORPORATES THE ELEMENTS of a successful learning program. We at UnCommon Golf plan to make this the standard in golf instruction in years to come. Unfortunately, today, most golfers are self-taught and have the same misconceptions as J.B. and Brian. Some who have ventured to take lessons have been disappointed by situations similar to J.B.'s experience with Jack Pierce.

Let me paint a picture for the future. You decide to take a lesson. You now decide to go to a qualified instructor that has been recommended to you. You ask your prospective instructor about his or her program, and you set goals together. Your short game is evaluated as well as your equipment. The goals are then made into a plan that is put into practice over the next couple of years. In the first few lessons, you learn the correct concepts and corresponding drills.

You then come for lessons on a regular basis to turn the concepts into habits. Your game improves in stages, and your handicap goes down. Your confidence grows, and you enjoy the game much more.

Now I'll let you in on a secret. Top instructors love seeing their students' improvement: when the light bulb goes on in the student's head after a concept is shown; when the slice turns into a draw; when the infuriating topped shot is replaced by solid impact; when a tension-filled hit is replaced by a rhythmic swing. These are the moments when the teacher knows why he took up golf instruction as a profession. We are sick of slices and scoops. They can be cured so easily.

Starting today, I challenge all the golfers who desire to get better to seek out the best instructor in their area. Judge them against the standards of Harry Wilkinson, and become very involved in your improvement process. I want to help you find your Harry Wilkinson!

Contact us at UnCommon Golf for a brochure about our instruction, and also to subscribe to our newsletter, *The Golf Advisor*.

I hope you enjoyed the book, and I'd enjoy getting feedback from you. Please contact me at:

UnCommon Golf
P.O. Box 181124
Casselberry FL 32718-1124
Toll-free (877) 901 KING
    or, locally, (407) 699-1184

Appendix A
Learning A Motor Skill

THROUGHOUT THE STORY THERE ARE REFERENCES to motor learning. This means learning something that requires movement of the hands, arms, and/or body in a prescribed way. As you will see from the comparisons, there are universally accepted steps of motor learning until we reach golf. The following are accepted steps for motor learning for various activities and sports.

Baseball:
- Make the team.
- Go to scheduled practices.
- Learn the basic skills (catching, hitting, throwing).
- Do drills so basics become second nature.
- Continue the process throughout your playing career.

Music:
- Find a qualified instructor.
- Take regular lessons.
- Learn the basics.
- Practice between lessons.
- Learn in a progression from simple to complex.

Martial Arts:
- Find a teacher, known as a master.
- Go to class several times a week.
- Learn in groups.
- Learn basic stances and mental approach.
- Progress from white belt to black belt.

When we turn to golf, we see a deviation from the pattern established in the learning of baseball, music, martial arts and many other endeavors. There are two approaches to golf. The first is the more common one, so I call it Common Golf. The second, more sensible approach, I call UnCommon Golf.

Common Golf

- Go to a driving range with a friend who plays a little better than you.
- From this friend, take advice such as "Keep your head down," "Keep your left arm straight," and "Take the club straight back and straight through."
- Try out tips from your friends.
- Use your driver and hit multiple buckets of balls so that these habits are ingrained.
- Buy new clubs and gadgets hoping they will cure your problems quickly.

UnCommon Golf

- **Find a qualified instructor.**
- **Take regular lessons.**
- **Learn the basic skills, such as face control, path, centered hits, grip, aim, set-up, putting, chipping**
- **Do drills, so that basics become second nature.**
- **Practice correctly between lessons.**
- **Learn in a progression from simple to complex and make improving an ongoing process.**

If the Common Golf example seems all too familiar to you, you need to try the UnCommon Golf approach. This process was promoted throughout the story, and it follows the logical process of learning any motor skill.

Appendix B
Club Fitting
Would You Wear Shoes That Didn't Fit?

I THINK MOST OF US HAVE A PAIR OF SHOES THAT WE REGRET buying. It didn't take long for us to realize that we had made a bad purchase; the blisters on our feet reminded us daily. When we go to purchase a pair of shoes, we look at size, width and style. Before buying we try them on.

In like manner, when we buy clubs, we should "try them on," in a process called club fitting. The main elements to take into account are lie angle, shaft flex, shaft length, design of the clubhead, grip size and kick point of the shaft. Here we will consider lie angle, shaft flex and shaft length.

Lie Angle

This is the most important of all the variables. As golfers, all of us respond to the shape of our ball flight and whether it goes to the target. If the ball doesn't go to the target, we make adjustments.

We find a way (even if it's not very effective) to get the ball to go to the target. The illustrations show the effect of incorrect lie angles. If you have clubs that are too upright, the ball will go more left, even when the leading edge is perpendicular to the target line. The opposite is true if your clubs are too flat.

You can check your lie angles by putting black electrical tape on the bottom of your clubs and hitting balls off a lie board or a piece of plywood. This will make a mark on the club and show you whether the club is the correct lie angle for your swing.

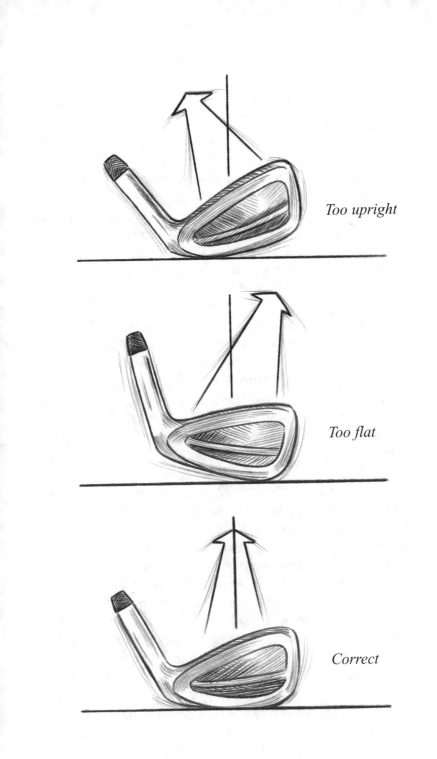

Too upright

Too flat

Correct

Let's consider two philosophies of club fitting. The first is that you should fit your clubs to match your current swing. This makes sense if you are not going to change your swing. The other philosophy is that clubs should fit your developing swing, taking into account how your swing is going to improve.

Most swings are from out-to-in and steep, which makes the mark on the tape more toward the toe. If you were fitting for your swing, you would need very upright lie angles. If, however, you were working to shallow out your swing, you would want your lie angle to be different, as well.

Shaft Flex

Deciding on the shaft flex is done best through experimentation. Having a chance to hit balls with various flexes is a must, so that you can get a feel for different shafts. Generally speaking, a stiffer shaft should be used by golfers with high clubhead speed; more flexible shafts are ideally used by golfers with less clubhead speed. Anyone who tells you which shaft you should use without watching your ball flight is just guessing . . . and, probably, trying to sell you a set of clubs.

Shaft Length

Shaft length can be a big factor for extremely tall or short people. The trend in the last few years has been to give people longer clubs. One of the big reasons for this practice is that the longer the shaft, the more clubhead speed. Manufacturers have delofted irons and lengthened clubs to increase a golfer's distance. Many times, however, this has been a smoke screen, a way to get golfers to buy new equipment.

The bottom line is this: you need to find a clubfitter in your area and experiment with shaft length and shaft flex before you make your buying decision. Look for a clubfitter who is also a good teacher, one who will take swing factors into account. Buying clubs is like buying shoes; you should try them on before you purchase them.

For more information and an e-mail response about clubfitting, visit our website at www.uncommongolf.com.

Appendix C
Finding Your Harry Wilkinson

OUR TEACHER IN THE STORY, HARRY WILKINSON, IS A MODEL for what a golf instructor should be. He exemplifies the qualities that most of us are looking for in a coach. But how do you find your Harry Wilkinson?

Use the criteria listed in Chapter 5 as a checklist and rate your prospective instructor accordingly. If he does most or all of the things on that list, he's hired. If not, keep looking until you find someone who does.

This search will pay great dividends as time goes on, for it will enable you, your children and your friends to enjoy a lifetime of better golf.

Questions to Ask Before Choosing an Instructor
- Do you teach full-swing and short game?
- Do you help with the mental side of the game?
- How long have you been teaching and what is your background?
- Do you have a money back guarantee?
- Will you allow me to have a trial lesson before I decide?

For more information and an e-mail response about finding your Harry Wilkinson, visit our website at
www.uncommongolf.com.

Appendix D
Answers to Frequently Asked Questions

AREN'T MOST GOLFERS SELF-TAUGHT?

Some well-known champions were basically self-taught, but that doesn't mean it is a model to which one should aspire. A high percentage of golfers drop out of golf every year because of the frustration of bad results from bad information. Being self-taught has not been successful for most golfers, judging by the great percentage of golfers who slice and the high nationwide handicap. A good instructor can cut the learning process down by a huge amount of time and make the process seem do-able.

I'VE READ A LOT OF ARTICLES, and they seem to contradict each other. I'm confused. What should I do?

The answer may sound like a broken record, but the fact is that a motor skill requires feedback to enable you to know whether you are doing it right. Articles can seem to contradict because of their context, and they cannot provide the needed feedback as to whether you are correctly doing the fundamentals discussed in the article.

GOLF INSTRUCTION IS TOO EXPENSIVE. How can I afford it?

Instruction is, typically, no more expensive than the equipment. If you are going to spend $300-$1000 for a set of clubs, you should be willing to spend an equal amount learning how to use them. Another thing you can do is get a friend or friends to take small group lessons with you and work out a price break with the instructor. You get a little less individual attention, but you make up for it with practice partners who know what you're working on.

HOW CAN I GET MORE INFORMATION about UnCommon Golf?

The good news is that this book and its information is an ongoing process that is taking place on the World Wide Web. Come to our website at

www.uncommongolf.com

to get Harry's Words of Wisdom, more answers to frequently asked questions, and an e-mail response to your questions. You'll also find the best support in the industry to help you reach your goals as a golfer. When you use the Internet, all of this is available 24 hours a day, 7 days a week.

Come join us as we work together to truly enjoy the process of playing this game better.

Appendix E
The Christmas Tree Effect
by Bradley Turner, PGA TGAS Golf Director

WHEN THE HOLIDAY SEASON APPROACHES, we all look forward to spending time with family and friends. It is a wonderful time to gather around the Christmas tree and share gifts with each other. In that spirit, I would like to share a gift of understanding with you, something I call the Christmas Tree Effect. I have been playing this wonderful game of golf for over 25 years and have been a golf professional for 15 years. During this time I have had many people express to me the famous phrase "I've got it!" I personally have said it 619 times to date; however, I do believe that I will get it for good the next time. I'm sure of it. What I would like to give you for Christmas is the reality of "I've got it!"

Every Christmas tree has a trunk, which I will call the crossover point. The crossover point can be described as the "I've got it" stage of skill development. The trunk ascends to the top, where we find a star which will represent the "I've got it, and I will prove that I have it" stage. This is where we all want to be, but few truly understand how to get there. Most golfers are looking for the quick fix or tune up lesson before the club championship, thinking that a $25 lesson entitles them to the first place trophy. Unfortunately, they never ascend the Christmas tree and will forever be stranded on the lower branches. They lack either the time or the desire to commit to such a journey.

The concept of this effect is much like the premise of trial and error. In order to change a slice into a controlled draw, a golfer must begin to develop a swing that will hook the ball severely at first. Live with the hook until the slice is forgotten. Then, relearn the slicing technique and use a smaller left to right shot. This is the essential part of skill development. We must continue to fine tune the shot patterns that we learn, and we must know them all. High, medium and low trajectory shots. Hooks, slices, fades and draws. Always keep fine tuning because the "I've got it!" will last for only a short period of time.

The Christmas Tree Effect might seem like a funny name that has nothing to do with golf, but it came while I was teaching a class at the Golf Academy of the South. I was explaining the concept that you just read about, and as I drew the diagram of it on the board, a student raised his hand and said, "That looks like a Christmas Tree." That term has been used ever since at the Golf Academy and has made a big difference in the students' understanding of changing their ball-flight. Now when a person who is getting rid of a slice hits the big hook that the teacher showed him, he just says "I'm going across the Christmas tree."

To illustrate true skill development, we will take the typical bogey golfer who hits the ball with a tremendous slice.

Stage 1. The chronic slicer.

Stage 2. Exaggerate the "hook" technique to learn the "primary hook."

Stage 3. As you move back over the crossover point, the ball flight begins to fade off too often. A definite preference for the left to right shot vs. right to left. Lack of confidence to hit a draw shot because of resulting pull hook.

Stage 4. Again we move over the crossover point and find the ball flight to be a "controlled hook." This appears to be desirable but will result in some sweeping hooks and many pushed drives.

Stage 5. At this stage the ball is under control with a preference for a fade. Capable of controlled draw shots at times but an occasional pull hook will occur.

Stage 6. The Ball Flight is controlled with a preference for a draw. The golfer is capable of fading the ball but on occasion hits this shot left to right.

Stage 7-10. During these stages, fine tuning of the path and face angle occur. This will only happen with hours upon hours of practice. Ball flight will become more controlled and scoring will drop considerably (assuming the player has a quality short game).

The time frame of skill development is dependent on a few things:

1) athletic ability,

2) desire and practice,

3) instruction and practicing correctly, and

4) fear of the unknown/psychological.

Fear of the unknown will cause many people to be complacent with their skill development. DO NOT fall into this suffocating trap. Next time you reach the crossover point by saying "I've got it," don't be afraid to go to the next stage. If you have the courage to crossover the crossover point, your time frame in your skill development will shorten. Cross over as soon as possible and as often as possible. When you allow yourself to do this you will be fine tuning a great golf game, your own!

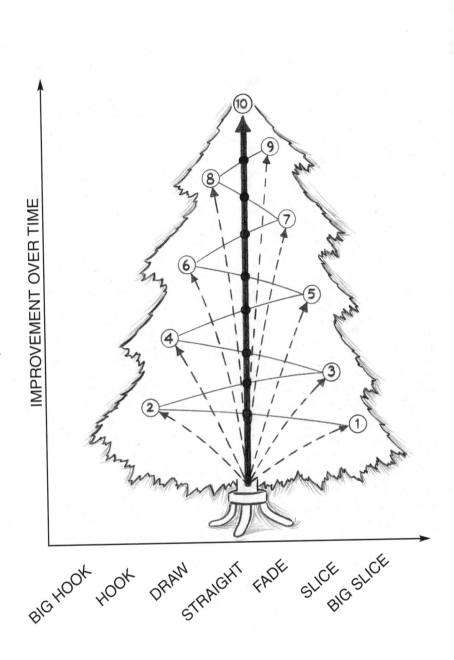

IMPROVEMENT OVER TIME

BIG HOOK   HOOK   DRAW   STRAIGHT   FADE   SLICE   BIG SLICE

Yes! I want to play the best golf possible! Please send

You're NOT Lifting Your Head, ISBN # 0-9674010-0-3, to help get me started.

Please send _____ copies @ $15.00 for a subtotal of _____

Florida residents please add 6% sales tax _____

S & H $3.00 first book. $1.00 each additional book _____

TOTAL COST OF ORDER _____

Name_____

Phone Number_____Fax Number_____

E-mail Address_____

Billing Address_____

Shipping Address_____

____ Check or money order enclosed, made payable to:

UnCommon Golf

____ Please charge this order to my credit card:

___Visa ___MasterCard ___Discover ___American Express

Credit card # _____

Expiration Date _____

Signature, credit card order_____

Mail your order to: UnCommon Publishing
P.O. Box 181124
Casselberry FL 32718-1124

For credit card orders, **call toll free:** (877) 901-5464
or send this form by **fax:** 407-388-0373
or log on to our **website:** www.uncommongolf.com.

Author and golf professional Charlie King is available to make a personal appearance at a meeting of your organization. He will autograph books on these occasions. To schedule an appearance, please call toll free (877) 901-KING [5464] or, locally, (407) 699-1184.

Yes! I want to play the best golf possible! Please send

You're NOT Lifting Your Head, ISBN # 0-9674010-0-3, to help get me started.

Please send _____ copies @ $15.00 for a subtotal of _____

Florida residents please add 6% sales tax _____

S & H $3.00 first book. $1.00 each additional book _____

TOTAL COST OF ORDER _____

Name_____

Phone Number_____ Fax Number_____

E-mail Address_____

Billing Address_____

Shipping Address_____

____ Check or money order enclosed, made payable to:
UnCommon Golf

____ Please charge this order to my credit card:

____Visa ____MasterCard ____Discover ____American Express

Credit card # _____

Expiration Date _____

Signature, credit card order_____

Mail your order to: UnCommon Publishing
P.O. Box 181124
Casselberry FL 32718-1124

For credit card orders, **call toll free:** (877) 901-5464

or send this form by **fax:** 407-388-0373

or log on to our **website:** www.uncommongolf.com.

Author and golf professional Charlie King is available to make a personal appearance at a meeting of your organization. He will autograph books on these occasions. To schedule an appearance, please call toll free (877) 901-KING [5464] or, locally, (407) 699-1184.